Contents

Preface vii

Chapter 1. The Four Challenges of Legal Writing 1

Part One: The Sentence

Chapter 2. The Efficient Sentence 5

A. Keep Related Words Together 6
- Participial Phrases 8
- Prepositional Phrases 10
- Adverbs (Especially '*Only*') 12
- Double Subject-Blockers 13

B. Use Pronouns Unambiguously 17
- Personal Pronouns 17
- Possessive Pronouns 19
- Demonstrative Pronouns 19
- Relative Pronouns 20

C. Eliminate Unnecessary Words 22
- Excess Verbiage 22
- Nominalizations 25
- Adverbs 28
- Multiple-Negative Constructions 28

D. Add Necessary Words 30

E. Use Parallel Constructions 32

Chapter 3. The Persuasive Sentence 37

A. The End of the Sentence 38
1. Identifying the Most Important Idea 39
2. Moving Words to the End 44
Objects 45
Subjects 46
Verbs 47
Adjectives 48
Adverbs 49

B. The Beginning of the Sentence 50
1. Topic Identification 50
2. Sentence Connection 51
Lookback 51
Phrases and Subordinate Clauses 52
Logical Traffic Signals 53
3. Ordinals and Their Overuse 56

C. The Middle of the Sentence 58

Chapter 4. The Professional Sentence 61

Part Two: The Paragraph

Chapter 5. The Order of Sentences 71

A. Classifying Paragraphs According to Their Purpose 72
1. Instructional Paragraphs 73
2. Affirmative Paragraphs 73
3. Responsive Paragraphs 75

B. Starting Paragraphs: The "Starter Sentence" 78
1. Starter Sentences for Instructional Paragraphs 78
2. Starter Sentences for Affirmative Paragraphs 79
3. Starter Sentences for Responsive Paragraphs 81
The Target Sentence 81
The Denial Sentence 82
4. Starter Sentences–Examples 86

Sentence, Paragraph, Argument, Brief

Meeting the Four Challenges of Legal Writing

David N. Greenwald

AMERICAN BAR ASSOCIATION
Litigation Section

Cover design by Jill Tedhams/ABA Design

Printed in the United States of America.

29 28 27 26 25   5 4 3 2 1

A catalog record for this book is available from the Library of Congress.

Discounts are available for books ordered in bulk. Special consideration is given to state bars, CLE programs, and other bar-related organizations. Inquire at Book Publishing, ABA Publishing, American Bar Association, 321 N. Clark Street, Chicago, Illinois 60654-7598.

www.shopABA.org

5. False Exceptions 90
Argument Headers as Starter Sentences 90
False Paragraph Breaks 91

C. The Rest of the Paragraph 92
1. Varying Sentence Length 93
2. Reducing Sprawl 94

Part Three: The Argument

Chapter 6. The Order of Paragraphs 99

A. 'Teach' 104

B. 'Argue' 110
1. Place Legal Contentions Before Factual 110
2. Group Related Contentions Together 113
Related Legal Contentions 113
Related Factual Contentions 119
3. Placement of Factually Similar Cases 122
4. Rebuttal Placement 124
5. IRAC and Related Principles of Argument Organization 126

Part Four: The Brief

Chapter 7. The Order of Arguments 129

Chapter 8. The Table of Contents 137

A. Depicting the Decision Tree 137
1. State the Reason for Each Result 143
2. When Possible, Describe Parallel Arguments with Similar Syntax 144
3. Use the Passive Voice to Show Similarities or Differences 145
4. Use '*Should*,' Not '*Must*' 147
5. Avoid Compound Entries 147

B. Introducing Factual Context 149
1. Include Allusions to Facts 149
2. Use Descriptive Proper Nouns 151

Chapter 9. Background Statements 153

A. The Order of Words in a Sentence 156

B. The Order of Sentences in a Paragraph 157

C. The Order of Paragraphs in a Background Statement 160

D. The Order of Background Statements 169

Afterword: How to Get Better 173

Additional Materials

General References on Writing 177
A Classification System for Contentions 179
Index 185

Preface

The lawyer who writes briefs works under conditions other writers do not face. Unlike most professional writers, who write for audiences as large as they can attract, the lawyer writes briefs primarily for a single judge or perhaps a few appellate judges. These readers read because they have to, not because they want to. They read to evaluate, not to be educated or entertained. They often read very quickly or even skim. They are a very demanding audience.

The lawyer who writes briefs also has another, secondary audience: the adversary, a critic unlike any other. Unlike the ostensibly independent critics who evaluate the work of novelists and scholars, the adversary has ethical and fiduciary duties to find fault with everything the lawyer has written. Often the adversary has keen financial incentives to make those criticisms sting. Even worse, when the adversary prevails, the lawyer's client—yet a third audience but one not always equipped to evaluate a brief—will sometimes suspect it was the brief, not the merits of the dispute, that brought about the defeat.

The lawyer also writes briefs under tough practical constraints. Reporters working for daily or weekly publications face tight deadlines, but the lawyer must often file briefs on timetables that, after adjusting for the length, complexity, and research requirements of briefs, are similarly tight. And despite the complexity of many legal arguments, briefs are subject to strict word limits. These can constrain advocacy considerably, especially when the lawyer needs to present more than one argument.

All these things and others combine for a sobering conclusion: brief-writing is hard.

Many books try to make this unusual, difficult mode of writing easier. They often stress that good brief-writing is just like other good writing and draw parallels to fiction or journalism. Others focus on rules of composition that govern non-legal and legal writing alike, and many such universal rules indeed exist. But these books tend to be less helpful in identifying the many things that distinguish legal writing from other types of writing. More important, they may be less helpful in offering concrete advice for meeting the unique challenges brief-writing presents. While many offer generous advice on improving sentences—where the principles of good legal and non-legal writing converge—few devote sustained attention to the features of paragraphs that are unique to briefs; or to how to sequence those paragraphs within a single argument; or to how to sequence the arguments in a brief; or to how to sequence the narrative in a background statement. Yet how well the lawyer meets these linear, sequencing challenges will determine whether a brief will come off as cogent and persuasive or instead as rambling, confusing, or incoherent.

This book offers detailed help for meeting all these challenges with a unified, practical approach to brief-writing (hereafter, *legal writing*), informed by decades of writing and editing briefs and of teaching it at law firms. Chapter 1 describes the book's approach and summarizes what will follow. Here, in the remainder of this preface, I describe, for those who are interested, how I came to write this book and how I wrote it. Those who are not interested should go straight to Chapter 1.

* * *

Over the past three decades, I held several jobs that helped me learn about legal writing. After graduating from law school in 1993, I began my career in Chicago at the U.S. Court of Appeals for the Seventh Circuit as a clerk to Chief Judge Richard A. Posner. In his chambers, I read hundreds of appellate briefs, and before argument in each appeal, I discussed the briefs with him and my co-clerk, Larry Downes. My co-clerk and I also helped Judge Posner to research and edit his opinions, every word of which he wrote himself. As a judge, scholar, and public intellectual, Judge Posner commanded his computer's keyboard the way Duke Ellington or Alicia de Larrocha commanded the piano's. It was a wonderful way to begin a career in legal writing.

I then became an associate at Cravath, Swaine & Moore in New York, the nation's second-oldest law firm. There I spent most of my time writing briefs, which partners then edited. From their careful edits I learned enormously. After a few years there, I joined the Manhattan office of the U.S. Attorney's Office for the Southern District of New York, which prosecutes federal crimes committed in Manhattan and the Bronx. Although much of my work there comprised presenting testimony to grand juries and trying cases, a very substantial component consisted in writing, *e.g.*, oppositions to suppression motions, oppositions to motions to dismiss indictments, oppositions to discovery motions, oppositions to petitions filed by federal and state prisoners, sentencing memoranda, and appellate briefs. Through my work at Cravath and at the U.S. Attorney's Office from 1994 to 2000, I wrote a lot of briefs.

After a few years as a prosecutor, I was invited to return to Cravath, which I did, and I became a partner there a few years later. Writing briefs continued to be a staple of my daily professional life after I became a partner, but something changed: I now had to edit briefs as well. I had little experience in editing briefs other than my own. I found it difficult and challenging, more challenging than writing and certainly less fulfilling. But it was a challenge I had to meet, so I tried my best. I also felt a professional, even moral obligation to try to explain to the junior lawyers whose work I had edited why I had changed their words. From that, I discovered that I was seeing the same faults over and over. I found that the four or five most common errors in sentence, paragraph, argument, and brief organization accounted for the vast majority of the edits I was making and that I could categorize the errors in ways that could help me edit faster and provide more instructive comments.

At around the same time, my firm tasked me with overseeing and developing Continuing Legal Education courses (state-mandated training for practicing lawyers) suitable for the firm's litigators. One of the courses I developed focused on editing sentences. As a nod to my years as a prosecutor, I called the course *Sentencing Guidelines*. In the ensuing years, I expanded the course to cover the paragraph, the argument, and the brief. I called this broader course *Legal Writing: A One-Dimensional Approach*, not because I intended it to be simplistic but because I conceived of writing as optimizing the linear array of words. I taught these courses for many years at my own firm. Then, after I retired and to support non-profit organizations, I started teaching variants of the course at law firms around the country.

In time, and as I started to publish articles describing aspects of my approach, I was encouraged to arrange my thoughts in a book. So I did. It wasn't hard. Or at least it wasn't as hard as writing any of the innumerable dismissal motions, summary judgment briefs, claim construction briefs, *Daubert* motions, motions in limine, motions to compel, post-trial motions, appellate briefs, motions opposing extensions, etc., I had to draft or edit during my nearly three decades as a litigator. After I had completed a polished draft, I shared it with some former colleagues and with some other lawyers and judges. Invigorated by their many insights, I prepared the final draft that you are now reading.

In the course of writing this book, I read over 100 randomly selected briefs filed over the past few years in state supreme courts and the U.S. Supreme Court. I chose to read briefs filed in high appellate courts rather than lower courts because, all other things being equal, lawyers devote more attention to briefs filed in higher courts than in lower; for many, filing a brief in a supreme court is a once-in-a-lifetime experience. I wanted to find a random selection of briefs at their best. That exercise gave me a broad view of the state of legal writing in the early 2020s. It also confirmed for me much of what I had been doing and teaching for the past three decades and suggested some things to add. From that exercise emerged the majority of the examples this book presents. The rest consist of examples I developed for this book. To avoid bias, no example comes from any brief I wrote or edited or from any brief submitted in any case in which my firm participated. Together with its unifying focus on word sequence, this book's abundance of before-and-after examples, nearly all drawn without attribution from filed briefs, sets it apart from the many other books in this field. I hope the examples help you learn from the most painless mistakes: the anonymous mistakes of others.

This book occasionally draws comparisons with literature or borrows insights from linguistics. I hope they are engaging and help you better absorb the lessons I am trying to teach. I do not want them to distract from the book's exclusively practical focus: writing and editing clear, well-organized briefs. If you can produce a brief that is clear and well organized, you will have made the brief 80–90 percent as effective as it can be. Additional touches of class, style, and even flair can make a really good brief into a great one, but only if the brief is already clearly, persuasively, and professionally written and sensibly organized.

This book is certainly intended for the beginning writer: the law student or the young lawyer who has not yet had a chance to write many briefs. But it is also intended for the experienced lawyer who has to edit briefs and give feedback to the drafters. Writing, editing, and giving feedback on writing are distinct skills. Many who are good at one are not good at the others. I believe that even excellent legal writers can find in this book articulations of things they do instinctively. Perhaps those articulations will help them as they try to help other lawyers become better writers.

I thank John Beerbower, Rolin Bissell, Roger Brooks, Richard Clary, Samuel Danon, Larry Downes, Ward Farnsworth, Stuart Gold, David Herman, John Martin, Gerald Masoudi, Paul Michel, John Paschetto, Chris Patton, Marc Rosenberg, and Paul Saunders for comments on drafts. I also thank Michelle Oberts and Richard Spencer of the American Bar Association and Bonnie Briggle of Lachina Creative for their help with the publication of this manuscript.

Chapter 1

The Four Challenges of Legal Writing

Writing is one-dimensional: it involves placing words on a page in a line. No matter how lengthy or complex, all writing consists of words arrayed consecutively in an order the writer chooses.

Of the choices the writer must make, word choice is the most basic. Word choice establishes, limits, and gives nuance to the content of a communication. But once the writer has chosen the words she wants to use, she faces the challenge of getting them in the right order. The grammar of the language she is using resolves many of those challenges, but even after grammatical rules are respected, the writer still has a lot of discretion over how to order the words she has chosen.

In legal writing, the sequencing challenges are four:

- the order of words in a sentence;
- the order of sentences in a paragraph;
- the order of paragraphs in an argument; and
- the order of arguments in a brief (or other document advancing a legal position).

Writing a good brief means meeting each of these four challenges. Each challenge is governed by entirely different principles, rules, and guidelines. This book describes all of them.

Here is a summary:

1. **The Order of Words in a Sentence:** A well-written sentence in a brief is *efficient*, *persuasive*, and *professional*. A sentence is efficient if it is easy for a judge to understand. A sentence is persuasive if its most impactful idea appears at the end of the sentence, and if the

two other regions of the sentence—the beginning and the middle—perform their distinct supporting roles. A sentence is professional if it is grammatical and reflects the usage conventions of U.S. litigation.

2. **The Order of Sentences in a Paragraph:** Paragraphs in an argument section of a brief fall into three categories: *instructional*, *affirmative*, and *responsive*. Each type of paragraph requires a well-constructed *starter sentence*. A good starter sentence can take various forms, but each must perform a core function dictated by the category of the paragraph that sentence leads off. Once a good starter sentence is in place, most of the remaining challenges of writing a good paragraph involve keeping the focus of the paragraph consistent and showing the relation between neighboring sentences. When those relations and the focus of the paragraph are clear, readers will say the paragraph reads well.

3. **The Order of Paragraphs in an Argument:** The challenge of ordering paragraphs in an argument is not linguistic or stylistic; it is analytic. One overarching principle, *Teach first–Argue later*, controls the process. A few other, subordinate principles, such as separating legal and factual arguments and grouping related arguments together, guide the aspects of the process that remain. To help apply the latter principle, this book proposes a formal classification system for determining the degree to which arguments relate to one another.

4. **The Order of Arguments in a Brief:** Ordering arguments in briefs that present several requires evaluating the arguments according to three parameters—*breadth*, *impact*, and *viability*—and then finding the sequence that places the stronger arguments, as assessed according to these parameters, before the less strong. The fundamental tool of brief organization is the outline, which ultimately becomes the brief's table of contents. Unlike tables of contents in other documents, the table of contents in a brief serves as a standalone summary of the document and also illustrates the logical relationships among its arguments. This book, in a separate chapter, explains how to help the table achieve those distinctive purposes.

This book takes up these four ordering challenges from smallest unit (sentence) to largest (brief), even though in practice, the last two challenges are tackled first, at the outlining stage, while the first two are met later, while drafting. The sequence of exposition also does not imply anything about the comparative complexity of the four challenges. In practice, the fourth and first challenges are generally the easiest to meet, whereas the second and third are the hardest. But with the help of this book, all the challenges should become manageable and lend themselves to reasoned discussion among colleagues. Even expert writers will find that the guidance this book offers will help them give feedback more useful than '*Try to make this brief better.*'

This book also includes a chapter on how to draft background statements, such as statements of fact or procedural histories. Drafting these important components of briefs draws upon many of the same principles applied in drafting arguments, but some require modification in this context and others are just different.

In an afterword, this book offers guidance for becoming a better legal writer on your own, followed by a very short list of useful general references.

PART ONE: THE SENTENCE

CHAPTER 2

The Efficient Sentence

A good sentence in a brief is efficient, persuasive, and professional. The next three chapters describe how to give a sentence each of these attributes.

* * *

When a sentence is efficient, a reader understands it easily. Efficiency is a mark of all good non-fiction writing, but it is especially important for writing judges have to read. More perhaps than any other professional group, judges have to read a large amount of prose very rapidly. Sets of briefs rarely comprise fewer than 40 pages in total and often include voluminous appended materials from the record. Thus, the lawyer who serves up sentences that lend themselves to rapid reading is doing the time-pressed and sometimes grumpy judge a big favor.

Many lawyers, when asked what makes a sentence efficient, will say that it uses no more words than it needs. Yes, word count is a measure of efficiency, and pruning unnecessary words is a major aspect of editing. But the lawyer who thinks efficiency comes merely from making every sentence as short as possible has an incomplete concept of efficiency. A long sentence can be easy to follow if the writer understands the other things that make sentences efficient. And the variety and complexity of the ideas legal writing expresses are such that the lawyer who writes only short sentences will generate a brief that is, paradoxically, harder to read than a brief by a lawyer who wields the delete key as only one of several efficiency-enhancing tools.

If the words in a sentence express their intended meaning, you have only three ways to make the sentence more efficient. You can (1) move words; (2) eliminate words; or (3) add words. These exhaust the possibilities because writing is linear; there are only so many things you can do to a line of words.

The three options give rise to the following five rules for enhancing the efficiency of a sentence:

1. Keep Related Words Together (Option 1);
2. Use Pronouns Unambiguously (Option 1);
3. Eliminate Unnecessary Words (Option 2);
4. Add Necessary Words (Option 3); and
5. Use Parallel Constructions (Options 1–3).

Disregarding these rules reliably yields sentences readers describe as turgid, muddy, unclear, and too long even when some of them are not too long. These five rules, unlike many discussed in this book, are not unique to legal writing, and none is controversial. The first, third, and fifth appear in all good English style guides, and the second and fourth are, to some extent, self-evident. The rules nonetheless warrant special discussion in the context of legal writing because the complexity of legal arguments tends to make violations more common and more consequential.

Let's consider each rule:

A. Keep Related Words Together.

More than many other languages, English relies on the proximity of words and phrases to each other to specify meaning. This is clearest for adjectives and nouns. If you write '*The dog chased brown the fox*,' this simple sentence will remain unclear no matter how many times you read it—*Is the dog or the fox brown?*—even though the same sequence of words in some languages will be comprehensible. In English, keeping adjectives next to the nouns they describe is so important a principle that native speakers will do it by instinct. They will never get it wrong.

Not so for words and phrases other than adjectives and nouns. Take, for example, this verse from the ghost scene of *Hamlet*:

> *'Tis given out that, sleeping in my orchard,*
> *a serpent stung me.*

Because English, unlike many other languages, does not have suffixes to show the noun (*a serpent? me?*) to which the participle, '*sleeping*,' relates, English relies instead on proximity to show the relation. Here, because '*sleeping*' is closer to '*serpent*' than to '*me*,' the sentence oddly implies that a serpent reportedly bit Hamlet's father while the serpent was asleep. English uses proximity to relate not only adjectives and participles to nouns but also verbs to adverbs, adverbs to adjectives, and prepositional phrases to nouns, verbs, and participles. The dependence of English on proximity gives rise to this fundamental rule of sentence efficiency: *keep related words together.*[1]

Shakespeare's misplacement of a participial phrase is not serious because he was writing words to be spoken, not read. In speech, the rule to keep related words together doesn't rigorously apply because the speaker can, through stress, timing, pitch, and volume, demonstrate relations between words and phrases that lie far apart from each other. None of those tools is available to the writer; proximity is the only tool she has. Clear relations between words and phrases are especially important for lawyers. Even the slightest ambiguity will cause the speed-reading judge to pause, if only for a fraction of a second, to use contextual clues to figure out what the lawyer intends to say. In nearly all instances, context will clarify the meaning, but why slow her down? Always be on the lookout for words and phrases that have straggled away from the words to which they relate, and shepherd them back into the fold.

In legal writing, related words most often separate from each other in sentences with

- participial phrases;
- prepositional phrases; or
- adverbs.

1. *See, e.g.*, William Strunk, Jr. & E.B. White, The Elements of Style 20–31 (Pearson 4th ed. 2000).

Since most sentences contain at least one of these constituents, separation can often occur. A different setting in which related words often separate from each other is what this book will call *double subject-blockers*. Double subject-blockers are not common, but they are more common in briefs than in other types of writing. Here is how to keep related words together in each of these four settings:

✦ Participial Phrases

Participial phrases that have separated from the words to which they relate become easier to spot when you appreciate that participles are simply verbs that have become adjectives: *e.g.*, a *pending* appeal, a *filed* brief, a *foregone* conclusion, a *reversed* decision. Just as you would never separate an adjective from the noun it describes, so too you should not separate a participle from the noun it describes. That is easy and natural for standalone participles ('*the dripping faucet*'). When, however, the participle does not stand alone but leads off a phrase ('*sleeping in my orchard*'), some separation of the participle from the described noun (Hamlet's father) may be inevitable. But you must keep it to a bare minimum by placing the participial phrase either immediately before or immediately after the noun the participle describes. Revise:

> ***Rather than excluding the confession***, *the prosecutor received permission from* **the court** *to offer it in evidence.*

to:

> ***Rather than excluding the confession***, ***the court*** *permitted the prosecutor to offer it in evidence.*

Misplaced participial phrases can appear at any place in the sentence, not just the beginning. The misplaced participial phrase at the end of the following sentence:

> *The session court reviewed the judgment* ***sitting in its appellate capacity****.*

can move to several places:

> *The session court,* ***sitting in its appellate capacity****, reviewed the judgment.*

or:

> ***Sitting in its appellate capacity****, the session court reviewed the judgment.*

Or, for different emphasis:

> *The judgment was reviewed by the session court* ***sitting in its appellate capacity****.*

As these examples show, a participial phrase, when correctly placed, can precede or follow the described noun.

Note one common legal context in which participles that don't describe a nearby noun appear to be acceptable:

> ***Applying these cases****, the judgment should be upheld.*

> ***Even crediting the Defendant's argument****, the complaint should not be dismissed.*

Since judgments do not *apply* cases and complaints do not *credit* arguments, the participles in these sentences, to use the grammarian's term, dangle. But the legal profession tolerates the dangling participles because they so clearly refer to the judge to whom the brief is addressed. There will be contexts in which, either for emphasis or to avoid even the slightest tone of a directive ('*Applying these cases*, **the Court should** *uphold the judgment.*'), you will want to dangle a participle in this way at the small expense of unimpeachable grammar.[2]

---

2. *See* H.W. Fowler, A Dictionary of Modern English Usage 674–76 (Oxford Univ. Press 1944) ("Unattached Participles: . . . [I]t is to be remembered that there is a continual change going on by which certain participles . . . acquire the character of prepositions or adverbs, no longer needing the prop of a noun to cling to; we can say *Considering the circumstances you were justified* . . . and need not correct into *I acquit you*. . . . [I]t is only fanatical purists who will condemn such sentences."); Bryan A. Garner, Garner's Modern American Usage 217 (Oxford Univ. Press 2003) ("Danglers: Some danglers, though, are acceptable because of long-standing usage. Examples are easy to come by: 'Considering the current atmosphere in the legislature, the bill probably won't pass.' . . . Any number of present participles have been used as conjunctions or prepositions for so long that they have lost the participial duty of modifying specific nouns."). *Cf.* H.W. & E.G. Fowler, The King's English 119 (Oxford Univ. Press 3d ed. 1931) ("The unattached or wrongly attached participle is one of the blunders most common with illiterate or careless writers. But there are degrees of heinousness in the offense.").

✦ Prepositional Phrases

Prepositional phrases are phrases that begin with prepositions: *in*, *to*, *for*, *by*, *on*, *of*, *under*, *with*, *beyond*, *beside*, *along*, *inside*, etc. Prepositional phrases provide details about nouns, verbs, or participles (*i.e.*, in participial phrases):

> *The year* ***of the conviction****.*
>
> *The jury deliberated* ***for four days****.*
>
> *Having offered* ***into the record*** *the exhibit, the lawyer concluded his examination.*

Because prepositional phrases have the grammatical capacity to relate to so many different types of words, they frequently end up in places where they generate unintended meanings. Sometimes the result is humorous, as in this Groucho Marx joke:

> *I shot an elephant in my pajamas. How he got in my pajamas I'll never know.*

But in legal writing, misplaced prepositional phrases tend to be only confusing. As written:

> *He would periodically review trades in the stocks in which the specialists made markets* ***for unusual activity****.*

is nonsensical. What are '*markets for unusual activity*'? Fix the misplacement by resettling the final prepositional phrase close to the word to which it relates:

> *He would periodically review* ***for unusual activity*** *trades in the stocks in which the specialists made markets.*

Or consider the following sentence:

> *Each employee was responsible for ensuring that he obeyed the rules,* ***from trading assistant to CEO****.*

To avoid an absurd, distracting implication (*How can a rule be a trading assistant?*), revise the sentence to:

> *Each employee,* ***from trading assistant to CEO****, was responsible for ensuring that he obeyed the rules.*

Sometimes choosing where to place a prepositional phrase takes a bit of thought. Consider the following sentence:

> *The court issued its decision holding the officer liable for the unlawful arrest of John Doe* **in 2018**.

Is the prepositional phrase '*in 2018*' correctly placed? It depends on what you mean.

If you mean that the court issued its decision in 2018, then the phrase is in the wrong place. Place the phrase closer to the words to which it relates: '*the court issued its decision*.' You can do this in a few ways:

> **In 2018**, *the court issued its decision holding the officer liable . . .*

or:

> *The court,* **in 2018**, *issued its decision holding the officer liable . . .*

You could even consider placing '*in 2018*' here:

> *The court issued its decision* **in 2018** *holding the officer liable . . .*

That placement also puts '*in 2018*' close to the words to which the phrase relates. But at the same time, it separates the participial phrase '*holding the officer liable . . .*' from the word to which it relates, '*decision*.' So this placement is not good. The other two are better.

But what if, instead, you mean that the arrest, not the decision, occurred in 2018? Then the sentence as originally written:

> *The court issued its decision holding the officer liable for the unlawful arrest of John Doe* **in 2018**.

is fine. But you might prefer to reverse the order of the two final prepositional phrases:

> *The court issued its decision holding the officer liable for the unlawful arrest* **in 2018** *of John Doe*.

When two or more prepositional phrases ('*in 2018*,' '*of John Doe*') relate to the same word ('*arrest*'), you have to choose which to place closer to that word. That choice is generally dictated by where you want to place emphasis, a topic taken up in the next chapter.

The hard thing about misplaced prepositional phrases is spotting them. Once spotted, they are always easy to fix.

✦ Adverbs (Especially '*Only*')

Adverbs describe verbs and adjectives. When describing adjectives, they always appear directly in front of the adjective they describe ('*uniquely powerful,*' '*invariably correct*'). When describing verbs, they generally appear immediately before or after the verb, as in the preceding sentence (restated for emphasis immediately below):

> *When describing adjectives, they* ***always*** *appear* ***directly*** *in front of the adjective they describe.*

Adverbs can tolerate some separation from the verb if the writer wants to give the adverb some special emphasis:

> *The Supreme Court reversed the decision* ***unanimously***.

Note, however, that this exception proves the rule; the separation is tolerable only because it's minimal. The following sentence does not read well:

> *The Supreme Court reversed the decision concerning the Harris Act* ***unanimously***.

In legal writing, the most commonly misplaced adverb by far is '*only*.' This is not merely because '*only*' is one of the most common adverbs but also because '*only*' is a very common adjective too ('*the only reason,*' '*the only thing*'). Because it can wear these two hats, it nearly always has the potential to describe more than one word in a sentence.

Consider the following sentence:

> *The directors only discussed the proposed acquisition.*

Does '*only*' appear together with the word to which it relates?

If '*only*' is functioning as an adverb describing the verb '*discussed*' (*i.e.*, the directors only *discussed* but did not *vote on* the proposed acquisition), then it appears in the right place, before '*discussed.*'

But if you want '*only*' to describe the acquisition—as opposed to, say, an unrelated labor contract—it's not in the right place. For that role, '*only*' should appear in front of '*the proposed acquisition*':

> *The directors discussed only the proposed acquisition.*

And if you want '*only*' to describe the directors (as opposed to, say, the officers), '*only*' must appear before '*the directors*':

> *Only the directors discussed the proposed acquisition.*

If a non-legal writer wants to move '*only*' away from the words it describes for rhythmic purposes or to better track the patterns of everyday oral speech ('*I only want three sandwiches.*'), that is not a big deal. But in legal writing, the misplacement of '*only*' should be avoided. Even slight misplacements that are not confusing can nonetheless slow a judge down.

> *The executive can only exercise its discretion in favor of non-citizens who satisfy the requirements of Section 1203.*

is clear enough, but the more careful writer will improve the aerodynamics of the sentence by revising it to:

> *The executive can exercise its discretion only in favor of non-citizens who satisfy the requirements of Section 1203.*

For the point of this sentence is to emphasize the limited population of non-citizens for whom favorable discretion is authorized. Keep '*only*' close to that concept.

Before submitting any draft or filing any submission, search for every appearance of the word '*only*' and make sure it's in the right place. In time, correct placement will become instinctive, and you will come to appreciate how the marginal improvement increases reading speed and precision.

✦ Double Subject-Blockers

A sentence can become inefficient when more than one phrase or clause precedes the subject of its independent clause:

> *In 2018, although the court did not hold the officer liable for false arrest, it held him liable for unlawful arrest.*

The sentence is grammatical and unambiguous but unwieldy. Before the subject of the independent clause, '*it*,' appears, the reader has to wade through first a prepositional phrase ('*In 2018*') and then a subordinate clause ('*although the court did not . . .*'). That is unfortunate for two reasons.

For one thing, the basic syntax of English is what linguists call Subject–Verb–Object (SVO). English is an example of an SVO language. French, Italian, and Chinese are others. Unlike readers of a non-SVO language (*e.g.*, German or Latin), English readers want to see the subject of a sentence relatively early in a sentence, or else they start to get confused. Putting one phrase or one subordinate clause before the subject is fine and often an important way to make the logic of the sentence clear. But more than one can be problematic.

The other problem is that the subordinate clause ('*although the court . . .*') wedges many words between the prepositional phrase ('*In 2018*') and the words to which '*in 2018*' relates: '*the court held.*' Thus, the sentence does not keep its related words together. Whenever two phrases or clauses before the grammatical subject of an independent clause make a sentence hard to follow, you can always, with perhaps some minor conforming changes, move one somewhere else:

> *In 2018, the court held the officer liable for unlawful arrest,* ***but it did not hold him liable for false arrest****.*

Or more succinctly:

> *In 2018, the court held the officer liable for unlawful,* ***but not false, arrest****.*

Here is another example:

> *In Judkins v. HT Window Fashions, while the appeal was pending, the court required the infringer to recall all marketing materials.*

The adverbial clause, '*while the appeal was pending,*' describes the timing of the enjoined recall. Hence, it should relocate to appear next to the words about the recall:

> *In Judkins v. HT Window Fashions, the court required the infringer,* ***while the appeal was pending****, to recall all marketing materials.*

Or, depending on the desired emphasis:

> *In Judkins v. HT Window Fashions, the court required the infringer to recall all marketing materials* ***while the appeal was pending****.*

Both revisions accelerate the appearance of '*the court*' and put the adverbial phrase that had delayed it closer to the concept to which it relates: the recall.

Prepositional phrases about cases often wedge themselves into positions where they don't belong:

> *Although most immunities are generally limited, under Nixon v. Fitzgerald, a president's immunity from prosecution under the Supremacy Clause is broader than the immunity other federal officials enjoy.*

is particularly problematic. The placement of '*under Nixon v. Fitzgerald*' after a subordinate clause both delays the appearance of the grammatical subject ('*a president's immunity*') and may make the judge think, despite the preceding comma, that *Nixon v. Fitzgerald* holds that '*most immunities are generally limited.*' Fix that:

> *Although most immunities are generally limited, a president's immunity from prosecution under the Supremacy Clause is, under Nixon v. Fitzgerald, broader than the immunity other federal officials enjoy.*

The advice not to postpone the subject's debut by more than one phrase or clause is another example of advice non-legal writers will sometimes ignore. In literary sentences, the grammatical subject often remains backstage for quite a while:

> *Just before it was dark, as they passed a great island of Sargasso weed that heaved and swung in the light sea as though the ocean were making love with something under a yellow blanket,* ***his small line*** *was taken by a dolphin.*
>
> *Hemingway*, THE OLD MAN AND THE SEA

> *Some years ago—never mind how long precisely—having little or no money in my purse, and nothing particular to interest me on shore,* ***I*** *thought I would sail about a little and see the watery part of the world.*
>
> *Melville*, MOBY DICK

> *Once upon a time, in the middle of winter, when the snowflakes were falling like feathers from the sky,* ***a queen*** *sat at her window working. . . .*
>
> *The Grimm Brothers,* SNOW WHITE *(H.R. Hunt, trans.)*

For their intended audience—readers who have picked up a work at leisure; readers who want to savor verbal beauty; readers who are under no deadline to get to the last page—these sentences work well. But the prose rhythms and literary effects fiction writers seek to achieve through sentences like these are extraneous to legal writing because they are antithetical to its unique goal: helping a judge understand your arguments quickly. Letting the grammatical subject appear promptly advances that goal.

In rearranging sentences to accelerate the appearance of the grammatical subject, be aware of two exceptions. The first is *logical traffic signals*: words and phrases like *but, however, indeed, moreover, that said, to be sure, nevertheless*. For logical traffic signals to help show the reader how a sentence relates to the preceding, they always have to appear at or close to the beginning of a sentence. So you should not fret if they appear together with other phrases or clauses that precede the subject:

> *In 2018,* ***by contrast****, the court held the officer liable for unlawful arrest.*
>
> ***Similarly****, when the First Amendment was adopted, "exercise" meant some "labor of the body." S. Johnson, A Dictionary of the English Language (1773).*

The other exception is appositives: nouns or phrases that describe a noun. If an appositive is helpful, it should appear immediately after the noun it describes. If that noun appears in a phrase or clause preceding the subject of the main independent clause, so be it:

> *In 2018,* ***the same year in which the officer was convicted****, the court held him liable for unlawful arrest.*
>
> *Before the arraignment of John Doe,* ***the Defendant****, the prosecutor filed a superseding indictment.*

B. Use Pronouns Unambiguously.

Sometimes a well-written sentence is susceptible to more than one meaning. Such ambiguities often stem from pronouns, nouns that substitute for another noun. Most obviously, pronouns allow you to substitute a short word for a longer. More importantly, they help you show relations between ideas in a single sentence or in two neighboring sentences. They also help you make a sentence more complex and interesting without making it harder to follow. But sometimes they make the sentence mean something you do not intend. Let's consider the types of pronouns that most often generate ambiguity—personal, possessive, demonstrative, and relative pronouns—and how to use them unambiguously.

✦ Personal Pronouns

Personal pronouns (*he/him*, *she/her*, *it*, *they/them*) can make a sentence inefficient when they precede the noun for which they stand:

> *When* ***it*** *reversed the judgment,* ***the appellate court*** *remanded the action for a new trial.*

As the speed-reading judge comes to the second word of this sentence, a question momentarily arises: what is '*it*'? The answer comes once the judge gets past the comma three words later, but in the intervening fraction of a second, the judge has been distracted. Place the pronoun after the noun for which it stands:

> *When* ***the appellate court*** *reversed the judgment,* ***it*** *remanded the action for a new trial.*

A personal pronoun, especially one at the beginning of a sentence, can stand for a noun in the preceding sentence. But if so, the preceding sentence should not be too complex:

> ***Maine's exclusion*** *of sectarian options from its tuition assistance programs violates the Free Exercise, Establishment and Equal Protection Clauses.* ***It*** *does so regardless of whether the exclusion turns on the religious status of the excluded schools or the religious uses to which the assistance would be put.*

is fine. But the pronoun in the middle of the following passage places unnecessary strain on short-term memory:

> ***Maine's exclusion*** *of sectarian options from its tuition assistance programs violates the Free Exercise, Establishment and Equal Protection Clauses for the reasons Justice Gorsuch stated in Espinoza.* ***It*** *does so regardless of whether the exclusion turns on the religious status of the excluded schools or the religious uses to which the assistance would be put.*

There is a limit to how long you can expect a reader to hold on to a term ('*Maine's exclusion*') from the beginning of a preceding sentence.

Here is another example of a pronoun that creates a risk of ambiguity:

> *The defendants were represented by assigned counsel while they attended the conference.*

Most judges reading this sentence will conclude that '*they*' means '*the defendants*.' But the conclusion is not inevitable. Revise the sentence as follows:

> *The defendants were represented by assigned counsel while the defendants attended the conference.*

And if that reworking seems awkward because of the close repetition of '*the defendants*,' avoid the problem by recasting the sentence, not by tolerating an ambiguous pronoun:

> *While the defendants attended the conference, they were represented by assigned counsel.*

'*It*,' when used to stand for an abstract noun or proposition, often benefits from expansion to clarify the thing for which it stands:

> *Judicial review itself presents a problem.* ***It*** *is only compounded by the religious discrimination that results.*

should be revised to:

> *Judicial review itself presents a problem.* ***The problem*** *is only compounded by the religious discrimination that results.*

In this way, the small possibility that the judge might initially think '*It*' refers to '*judicial review*' never arises.

✦ Possessive Pronouns

The ambiguities personal pronouns sometimes generate may also arise in sentences with possessive pronouns: *his*, *her*, *its*, *their*. Even when possessive pronouns closely follow the noun they describe, they can make a sentence inefficient if they appear after more than one noun for which they could also stand:

> *When the appellate court reversed the district court's judgment, it also vacated* ***its*** *opinion.*

Here, the personal pronoun, '*it*,' unambiguously refers to the appellate court. (The possibility that '*it*' could refer to '*the judgment*' is too far-fetched to cause confusion.) But the possessive pronoun, '*its*,' is ambiguous because it follows two singular nouns, '*the appellate court*' and '*the district court*,' to which this possessive pronoun might refer. Most judges will understand from the context that the vacated opinion is the district court's, but why make them resort to context? Revise the sentence to eliminate the possessive pronoun altogether. There is no way to use it unambiguously:

> *When the appellate court reversed the district court's judgment, it also vacated* ***the district court's*** *opinion.*

Here is another example of an ambiguously placed possessive pronoun:

> *When non-citizens violate those rules, Congress has prescribed procedures for* ***their*** *removal.*

Although the context will resolve the ambiguity, it's better to avoid it altogether:

> *When non-citizens violate those rules, Congress has prescribed procedures for* ***the non-citizens'*** *removal.*

✦ Demonstrative Pronouns

Another source of potential ambiguity is demonstrative pronouns: *this*, *that*, *these*, *those*. The ambiguity generally arises from using the pronoun as a standalone noun rather than as an adjective:

> *Both the Secretary's implementing regulations and Section 5314 focus on filing reports, not on reporting each account.* ***This*** *is clear from several features of the implementing regulations.*

> *While the regulations require accurate reports stating transactional data for each "financial account,"* ***that*** *merely describes the substance of the reporting requirement and does not elucidate the definition of that term.*

To eliminate the ambiguity, convert the pronouns from standalone nouns to adjectives and add an appropriate noun:

> *Both the Secretary's implementing regulations and Section 5314 focus on filing reports, not on reporting each account.* ***This focus*** *is clear from several features of the implementing regulations.*

> *While the regulations require accurate reports stating transactional data for each "financial account,"* ***that requirement*** *merely describes the substance of the reporting requirement and does not elucidate the definition of that term.*

In some settings, a standalone demonstrative pronoun, used as a noun rather than as an adjective, can be rhetorically powerful:

> *Maine argues that its law will protect its coastline from erosion.* ***That*** *is not so.*

But using '*That*' as a standalone pronoun is effective only because its referent—the proposition that '*its law will protect its coastline from erosion*'—is absolutely clear.

✦ Relative Pronouns

Relative pronouns—primarily '*that*' and '*which*'—are another source of ambiguity, and, to return to a theme, that ambiguity is more serious in legal writing than in other writing. Most stylists call for distinguishing between relative clauses that define a noun by restricting or limiting it; and relative clauses that describe a noun non-restrictively or parenthetically. The stylists prescribe '*which*' for non-restrictive or parenthetical clauses (flanked by commas), and they prescribe '*that*' (without a preceding comma) for restrictive or limiting. That is the standard approach in the United States at least.[3]

---

3. *See, e.g.*, THE CHICAGO MANUAL OF STYLE §§ 5.25, 6.27 (Univ. of Chicago Press 17th ed. 2017); NEW OXFORD AMERICAN DICTIONARY 1980–81 (Oxford Univ. Press 2d ed. 2005); *but see* THE AMERICAN HERITAGE DICTIONARY, *that* (usage note) (Houghton Mifflin Harcourt 4th ed. 2006) ("[T]he use of *which* with restrictive clauses is common.").

To appreciate the distinction, compare the following examples:

> **Non-Restrictive/Parenthetical:** *The regulation,* ***which*** *the FDA promulgated in 2014, prohibited off-label marketing in direct consumer advertising.*

Here, the preceding discussion has presumably focused the reader's attention on the specific regulation under discussion. The only reason the writer has set off between commas the relative clause, '*which the FDA promulgated in 2014,*' is to give the reader more information about the regulation.

> **Restrictive/Limiting:** *The regulation* ***that*** *the FDA promulgated in 2014 prohibited off-label marketing in direct consumer advertising.*

Here, by contrast, the preceding discussion has presumably described a set of regulations, only one of which was promulgated in 2014. The relative clause restricts the subject of the sentence to the latter and hence defines it. For that definitional purpose, only '*that*' is appropriate.

Or consider the following sentence from a brief in a patent case:

> *In 2013, Robertson filed two continuation applications which included Claim 31.*

If you mean that Robertson filed only two continuation applications in 2013, then you should insert a comma before '*which*':

> *In 2013, Robertson filed two continuation applications, which included Claim 31.*

By contrast, if Robertson filed more than two continuation applications in 2013 but you want to focus on only the two including Claim 31, then you should change '*which*' to '*that*':

> *In 2013, Robertson filed two continuation applications that included Claim 31.*

The distinction between '*that*' and '*which*' is relatively recent. The best writers of the 19th century routinely used '*which*' restrictively:

> *[T]here is scarcely any horror which may not occur under it if the despot pleases.*
>
> *John Stuart Mill*, THE SUBJECTION OF WOMEN *(1869)*

Modern writers, especially British, still sometimes use '*which*' (without a comma) restrictively:

> *Wellington accepted absolutely that separation of feeling from function which had given birth to the modern state.*
>
> *John Keegan*, THE MASK OF COMMAND *(1987)*

Or they use it non-restrictively, but omit a preceding comma:

> *I saw George walk swiftly up to the doorman who stood under the red and white canopy which stretched out over the sidewalk.*
>
> *Roald Dahl*, VENGEANCE IS MINE, INC. *(1980)*

The U.S. lawyer should not be so flexible. There will be sentences in which the distinction matters. Make respecting the distinction a habit.

C. Eliminate Unnecessary Words.

Perhaps the most common advice for good writing is to eliminate unnecessary words.[4] This advice is so common and commonsensical as to be a platitude. If a word is not necessary, why use it? So long as your concept of necessity is broad enough to appreciate that you can need a word not just to convey content but to enhance prose rhythm or to permit a certain emphasis, then the principle is unimpeachable. But don't mistake this prescription for the also common, but bad, advice to *Keep sentences short*, or bromides like *Shorter is better*. A paragraph consisting of one short sentence after another will make for pretty tiresome reading. The better advice, at least in the context of standalone sentences, is to make sentences as long as, but no longer than, the complexity of their ideas requires. Eliminating unnecessary words is a critical part of that process.

✦ Excess Verbiage

Consider, for example, the following final sentence of an advisory memo:

---

4. *E.g.*, WILLIAM STRUNK, JR. & E.B. WHITE, THE ELEMENTS OF STYLE 23–24 (Pearson 4th ed. 2000) ("Omit needless words.").

> *For the foregoing reasons, we believe the better view under applicable law is that the proposed policy would be upheld as lawful under U.S. law.*

One can readily imagine why a young lawyer, eager to show off how well he has learned the dialect of Litigation English, would submit a draft with such an august peroration. The problem, however, is not its diction or style. For professional writing, they are fine. The problem is that the underlying idea is extremely simple, so simple that the 25-word sentence that embodies it is not commensurate with the simplicity of its thought. Compress it into the curt:

> *For these reasons, the proposed policy is probably lawful.*

A major source of excess verbiage in legal writing is throat-clearers or, more clinically, "metadiscourse."[5] Metadiscourse consists of prefatory phrases that self-consciously signify that the lawyer is aware she is writing for an audience or to oppose an adversary:

> *It should be noted/We note . . .*
>
> *It is respectfully submitted/We respectfully submit . . .*
>
> *It cannot be seriously contended . . .*
>
> *There is little reason to believe . . .*
>
> *It is little surprise that . . .*

Sometimes the best practice is to omit these phrases altogether. Other times, an adverb (*Surely*, *Notably*, *More importantly*, *Not surprisingly*) will achieve your purpose without the windup.

A very common phrase is '*There is*' or '*There are*.' Sentences may efficiently begin with this phrase to highlight a contrast with an idea in the preceding sentence.

> *No case holds that . . . . There is, however, case law describing . . .*

The effect of '*There is*' is to make '*however*' somewhat more impactful. Some writers may also like the rhythmic effect of leading off a sentence with two iambs ('*There* ***is***, *however*, . . .'). That is okay too.

5. *See* Joseph M. Williams, Style: Ten Lessons in Clarity and Grace 27–29 ("Metadiscourse: Writing About Writing") (Scott, Foresman 3d ed. 1989).

And there are other settings in which there is nothing wrong with using this basic English locution.

Sometimes, however, '*there is/are*' and its relative '*it is*' merely delay the appearance of the grammatical subject[6] and add a few words in the process. The sentence:

> *There are many cases that hold . . .*

should be revised to:

> *Many cases hold . . .*

Similarly,

> *There is no reason/It is not clear why this Court should . . .*

should become:

> *This Court should not . . .*

Be aware of other phrases where excess verbiage often lurks. Here is a list of phrases common in legal writing that you can always compress:

whether or not	→	*whether*
as to whether	→	*whether*
in the event that	→	*if*
notwithstanding that	→	*even though*
despite the fact that	→	*even though*
given that	→	*because*
by virtue of	→	*by/through*
at present	→	*now*
at this/that time	→	*now/then*
in no uncertain terms	→	*clearly*
in order to	→	*to*
for the purpose of [verb]*ing*	→	*to* [verb]

6. *See* Bryan A. Garner, Garner's Modern American Usage 331 ("Expletives"), 787 ("there is; there are[:] A. As Signals of Clutter") (Oxford Univ. Press 2003).

It is for this reason that	→	*This/That is why*
is able to/is capable of	→	*can*
expressly/explicitly states	→	*states*
plain language	→	*language/text*
in violation of law	→	*unlawful*
criminal violation	→	*crime*
each and every	→	*each* or *every*
stipulate and agree	→	*stipulate* or *agree*
with respect to	→	[almost anything else]

Like the verbal tic '*in terms of*,' '*with respect to*' indicts the writer for not having taken time to think through the idea a sentence is trying to express.

✦ Nominalizations

A nominalization is a noun that is derived from a verb (*declaration–declare*; *antagonism–antagonize*; *argument–argue*)[7] or from an adjective (*ability–able*; *kindness–kind*). Many have familiar endings based on their etymology: *-tion* (verbs with Latin roots); *-sis* (verbs with Greek roots); *-ment*, *-ance*, or *-ence* (verbs with French roots); *-ty* (adjectives with French roots); *-ness* (adjectives with Germanic roots). But many nominalizations have no common suffix: *e.g.*, proposal, gift, death, breach, lease, release. For this discussion, a gerund—a verbal form that functions as a noun ('the *rendering* of a decision')—qualifies as a nominalization as well.

Nominalizations come in for harsh criticism from stylists, and often rightly so. They are often the telltale sign of bureaucratic, academic, turgid, or generally weak prose. Here are examples of what the stylists are complaining about (nominalizations in bold):

> *The defendant's* ***ability*** *to file a motion to dismiss turns upon whether* ***service*** *of an answer has occurred.*

---

7. A more descriptive, less jargony term for this type of nominalization is a '*buried verb*.' Bryan A. Garner, Garner's Modern American Usage 117 (Oxford Univ. Press 2003).

> *The* ***difficulty*** *in the* ***reconciliation*** *of the cases stems from* ***differences*** *in their facts.*
>
> *The* ***interpretation*** *of this contract requires an* ***examination*** *of the* ***relation*** *among its various provisions.*

These sentences are grammatical and well formed. Indeed, their diction will strike most readers as highly professional, even erudite. Therein lies the problem. Lawyers, especially young lawyers, get into the habit of using nominalizations as these examples do precisely because they want to sound professional. For them, sounding professional means imitating diction that is regrettably common in academic, governmental, and scientific documents. Sometimes the inexperienced lawyer will incline to nominalizations from worry that the idea of the sentence sounds too simple to be impressive. So she will dress up the simple idea in nominalizations to try to enhance its heft.

Nominalizations are not inherently bad. In all writing on complex subjects, they play important roles, some explored in later chapters. No good piece of legal writing will avoid them entirely. But they can make a sentence seem listless. You can see this by rewriting the sentences above to eliminate all their nominalizations:

> *Whether the defendant can file a motion to dismiss turns upon whether the defendant has served an answer.*
>
> *It is difficult to reconcile the cases because they have different facts.*
>
> *To interpret this contract, the Court must examine how its various provisions relate to one another.*

By comparing the sentences, you will note that the revised use more verbs than the original. To most readers, the revised sentences will seem more energetic.

Getting rid of nominalizations can also make a sentence's verb more descriptive, which will also make the sentence seem more muscular:

> *He conducted a* ***deposition*** *of X.* → *He* ***deposed*** *X.*
>
> *She provided* ***advice*** *to X.* → *She* ***advised*** *X.*

He gave ***information*** *to X.*	→	*He* ***informed*** *X.*
She entered into an ***engagement*** *with X.*	→	*She* ***engaged*** *X.*
He filed ***suit*** *against X.*	→	*He* ***sued*** *X.*

These examples also reveal an added benefit of getting rid of nominalizations if the sole goal is to lower word count: eliminating a preposition the nominalization requires. Whenever the object of a sentence is derived from a verb, consider whether compressing the verb and object into a single, more specific verb makes the sentence better.

But if you are going to use nominalizations (as you often should), use them. Don't use '*the fact that*' instead, as in:

> ***The fact that*** *the statute does not strip district courts of jurisdiction over constitutional claims should resolve the question presented.*
>
> *But* ***the fact that*** *the rules turn on account balance rather than account number casts doubt on Defendant's contention.*
>
> *The government's position is premised on* ***the fact that*** *the statutory language appears in the singular.*
>
> ***The fact that*** *Camacho was not present in court for routine continuances does not establish* ***the fact that*** *he intended to be absent.*

Each of these sentences lazily uses '*the fact that*' to fuzz up the true topic of the sentence. Use nominalizations instead to restore the focus:

> *The statute's* ***failure*** *to strip district courts of jurisdiction over constitutional claims should resolve the question presented.*
>
> *But the rules'* ***dependence*** *upon account balance rather than account number casts doubt on Defendant's contention.*
>
> *The government's position is premised on the* ***appearance*** *of the statutory language in the singular.*
>
> *Camacho's* ***absence*** *from court for routine continuances does not establish that his* ***absence*** *was intentional.*

You can, and maybe should, revise some of these sentences further to eliminate the nominalizations. (*E.g.*, '*Just because Camacho did not attend court for routine continuances does not establish that he failed to attend intentionally*.') But just getting rid of '*the fact that*' improves their efficiency.

✦ Adverbs

When trying to get rid of unnecessary words, adverbs merit attention. Sometimes you will be told to eliminate adverbs from your drafts. Stated unqualifiedly, the advice is bad. Adverbs invest sentences with content, nuance, and richness other words cannot. They can even help to eliminate excess verbiage by replacing nominalizations, as in the sentence before the last. That sentence could have been written:

Stated without qualification, the advice is bad.

but some readers will find it not only a word longer but also more bureaucratic than the original sentence, which used '*unqualifiedly*.'

There is, however, a class of adverbs that deserve a cold eye: intensifying adverbs. Intensifying adverbs are adverbs like *very*, *greatly*, *vastly*, *abundantly*, *indisputably*, *unquestionably*, *categorically*. When these show up in drafts, ask yourself whether they can disappear. They sometimes can, and this will stabilize the mood of a sentence in a way that many judges will prefer.

✦ Multiple-Negative Constructions

Avoid constructions with multiple negatives. In its simplest form, this means not using flagrantly double-negative constructions like:

The plaintiff did ***not*** *allege that the defendant did* ***not*** *act negligently.*

Clearly, the sentence should be simplified:

The plaintiff alleged that the defendant acted negligently.

Yet double-negative constructions can be more subtle:

A change in a law should ***not*** *be presumed to be* ***meaningless****.*

> ***No** case holds that a finding of recklessness **cannot** be made on summary judgment.*
>
> ***Nothing** is left of defendant's contention that ICFA claims **cannot** be based on findings of negligence.*
>
> *The jury **declined** to find the defendant **not** guilty.*

And even triple- or quadruple-negative constructions are fairly common in briefs:

> *A **non-citizen** is **ineligible** for relief because she does **not** satisfy a **non-discretionary** eligibility requirement.*
>
> *The State **cannot** defend a rule that **rejects ineffective** assistance claims for **lack** of trial counsel testimony.*
>
> *The trial court did **not** plainly **err** in **failing** to act sua sponte to **exclude** the challenged testimony.*

It may be hard to purge multiple-negative constructions from your prose completely. Because juries do not find criminal defendants innocent, it will be wrong to call a not-guilty verdict a verdict of innocence. All criminal appellate lawyers will at some point have to assert that an error was '*not harmless beyond a reasonable doubt*.' Similarly, in a brief concerning a Sixth Amendment violation, eliminating the phrase '*ineffective assistance of counsel*' from all sentences in which another negative concept appears will not always be possible. But in general, when you start to see multiple-negative constructions, try to eliminate at least one of them. Most of the time you can do that, as in the following revisions of some of the earlier examples:

> *A change in a law presumptively carries meaning.*
>
> *To be eligible for relief, a non-citizen must meet every eligibility requirement.*
>
> *The State must acknowledge the infirmity of a rule that requires all ineffective assistance claims to be supported by trial counsel testimony.*

Complete elimination of multiple-negative constructions is not the goal. The goal is merely to minimize them so that they do not behave like speed bumps.

D. Add Necessary Words.

Sentences can seem turgid, bureaucratic, or otherwise unclear not because they are too long but because they are too short; because the writer, owing to laziness, confusion, or both, has failed to express them with enough words to make his thought transparent. Consider:

> *The statement can be explained by two things, both of which rest at the crux of this investigation.*

This sentence is only 18 words, below the 20-word average some writing authorities endorse. But it's not clear. The reason is not that the writer has used too many words. The reason is that the idea the writer is trying to express is moderately complex. To express it requires more words, not fewer:

> *To understand the statement, one must appreciate two things, both of which are critical to any balanced assessment of whether the Department should file charges.*

Perhaps the sentence as revised is not especially impressive or well constructed. You might find better ways to express its idea. But it's hard to argue that lengthening the sentence made it worse.

Or take the following sentence you could easily find at the outset of a draft research memorandum:

> *You have asked whether frustration of purpose may be successfully asserted under circumstances not specifically recited in a force majeure clause.*

This is a poor sentence for several reasons, but its fundamental flaw is that it is lazy. It tries to collapse a moderately complex thought into a sentence whose length cannot accommodate it. Here is a revision:

> *You have asked whether the defense of frustration of purpose may apply when a contract's force majeure clause does not recite as an excuse for non-performance the circumstance purportedly frustrating the contract's purpose.*

Longer, yes. But also clearer and more informative.

Of the five rules offered in this chapter, adding necessary words is probably the hardest to reduce to turnkey prescriptions. Verbal stinginess generally presents itself as a sentence that seems muddy or imprecise but that does not have any unnecessary words, unclear pronouns, or misplaced words or phrases. When you come across such a sentence, ask whether it is using a single noun or pronoun when a group of words would be more precise:

> *Because Thunder Basin cuts against the government, the government falls back on constitutional avoidance.*
>
> *No case considered whether probable cause would be met by the odor of marijuana had those states had odor-proof requirements.*
>
> *The court's discretion was sound for several reasons.*

Although most judges will get the gist, each sentence, as written, is imprecise. The only way to make each precise is to add words:

> *Because Thunder Basin cuts against the government's position, the government resorts to arguing that the court should construe the statute in a way that renders it constitutional.*
>
> *No case considered whether in states that require marijuana to be transported in odor-proof containers, the standard for probable cause would have been met if the arresting officer had detected in a vehicle the odor of that drug.*
>
> *The court's exercise of discretion was sound for several reasons.*

And when you use weak verbs like '*implicate*' or '*relate*,' ask whether you are using them as a veneer over incomplete expression:

> *Overruling Patterson would not* ***implicate*** *substantial reliance interests.*
>
> *Courts have also found a party to be in default when litigation misconduct* ***implicates*** *the courts' inherent powers.*
>
> *In its brief, the government recites the probable cause standard as it* ***relates*** *to warrantless searches of automobiles.*

These sentences should be revised to eliminate these verbal crutches:

> *Overruling Patterson would not undermine measures taxpayers have taken in reliance on its holding.*

> *Courts have also found a party to be in default when litigation misconduct is so serious that it makes it harder for the court to exercise its inherent power to oversee the case over which it is presiding.*
>
> *In its brief, the government recites the standard for whether an officer lacking a warrant has probable cause to search an automobile.*

Sometimes nominalizations, rather than attracting extra words around them (*e.g.*, prepositions), are a sign that words should be added. For example:

> *A reasonable-belief standard is also unworkable because of* ***the indeterminacy of the bounds of professional practice****.*

should be revised to:

> *A reasonable-belief standard is also unworkable because* ***the line that separates professional from unprofessional practice is often hard to draw****.*

Spotting verbal stinginess gets easier as you become more self-critical and less tolerant of sentences that do not quite say what you mean. As you develop this skill, you may find that editors who used to complain that your drafts were too wordy may become less hostile.

E. Use Parallel Constructions.

An important principle of efficient style is to use parallel constructions: to present coordinated ideas in similar form. A major reference articulates the principle in this way: "Every element of a parallel series must be a functional match (word, phrase, clause, sentence) and serve the same grammatical function in the sentence (*e.g.*, noun, verb, adjective, adverb)."[8] In some instances, you achieve parallel constructions by eliminating words; in others, by adding some. And in some, by just moving words around.

---

8. The Chicago Manual of Style § 5.242 (Univ. of Chicago Press 17th ed. 2017).

Mistakes in parallel construction often come from using correlative conjunctions:

> *both . . . and*
>
> *either . . . or*
>
> *neither . . . nor*
>
> *between . . . and*
>
> *not because . . . but because*
>
> *not only . . . but also*

Consider the following sentence:

> *This policy will result in* ***not only*** *the loss of harmful evidence* ***but also*** *potentially helpful evidence.*

The sentence is missing the words necessary to coordinate the two objects of '*result in*' in a parallel manner:

> *This policy will result in* ***not only*** *the loss of harmful evidence* ***but also*** *the loss of potentially helpful evidence.*

Now, with the principle of parallel construction respected, the good editor will realize that some unnecessary words can be pruned:

> *This policy will result in the loss of* ***not only*** *harmful* ***but also*** *potentially helpful evidence.*

Because the correlative conjunctions, '*not only*' and '*but also*,' appear before adjectives (*harmful*; *potentially helpful*), the sentence still respects the principle of parallel construction.

Here are subtler examples of non-parallel constructions, with the poorly coordinated terms in bold:

> *Like all negligence* ***cases****, a* ***claim*** *about a cow in a road requires evidence of negligence.*
>
> *Unlike* ***Nebraska law****,* ***the use of a screen*** *to protect a child witness is authorized by Florida law.*
>
> *There is no incompatibility between* ***FTC proceedings*** *and* ***district courts****.*

Here are properly parallel revisions:

> *Like all negligence* ***claims****, a* ***claim*** *about a cow in a road requires evidence of negligence.*

> *Unlike* ***Nebraska law****,* ***Florida law*** *authorizes the use of a screen to protect a child witness.*

> *There is no incompatibility between* ***FTC proceedings*** *and* ***district court actions****.*

Even more subtly non-parallel is the following sentence:

> *This allows serious cases to be pursued rather than devoting court resources to resolving minor offenses.*

The lack of parallelism here arises because the sentence has two different vantage points: the vantage point of the prosecutor and the vantage point of the judge. That is inherently confusing. Either make the vantage points of the two compared items identical:

> *This allows prosecutors to pursue serious cases rather than force them to devote their offices' resources to resolving minor offenses.*

or make the difference explicit and express it in parallel fashion:

> *This allows prosecutors to pursue serious cases rather than force judges to devote resources to resolving minor offenses.*

Another source of inefficient, non-parallel construction is verbs that take different prepositions. The tendency is to omit the first preposition:

> *For the following reasons, I disagree and dissent from the Court's opinion.*

The preposition '*with*' must be added:

> *For the following reasons, I disagree* ***with*** *and dissent from the Court's opinion.*

Or better, because a purist would say that one cannot disagree with an opinion but only with its reasoning:

> *For the following reasons, I disagree* ***with the reasoning of*** *and dissent from the Court's opinion.*

Although you need not go that far, paying attention to whether your sentences coordinate similar ideas in parallel fashion will give your prose a precision and balance that most readers will find classier and easier to read.

* * *

Despite all the well-founded complaints about legalese and lawyers' overuse of big words, faulty word placement and word count (sometimes too high; sometimes too low) more seriously undermine a sentence's efficiency. By focusing on these aspects of the sentences you write and edit, you will produce sentences that a judge can read at least more quickly. That is not everything, but it counts for a lot. A judge has many more briefs to read after she finishes yours. Help her get through the pile.

CHAPTER 3

The Persuasive Sentence

The general goal of non-legal writing is to inform or to entertain, not to persuade. Parables, polemical essays, and op-ed pieces qualify this general statement, but to some extent they also prove it sound, for most such works find themselves packaged with other, non-forensic works. If they were packaged alone, they would probably not win large audiences. Few people, when they pick up something to read, want to have their opinions changed. And *no one* reads briefs for pleasure.

Yet persuasion, not entertainment or instruction, is what lawyers get paid for. To be sure, and to foreshadow a theme that later chapters will take up, they get paid to teach as well: to teach a judge the facts of the case and the applicable law. But they do that only to advance their sole professional goal: to persuade a judge that their client is right.

Most of a lawyer's skill in persuasion comes from her knowledge of the law and her knack for playing to cognitive biases that may hide flaws in an argument. Relatedly, some of a lawyer's persuasive skill comes from her ability to choose words that have nuances or connotations likely to appeal to a judge's social or intellectual prejudices. These important and difficult aspects of psychology and word choice are beyond the scope of this book. But some persuasive force derives from how the lawyer organizes the words in a sentence. Here, this book can help a lot.

Understanding how word order can enhance persuasion begins with understanding the distinct roles each part of a sentence plays—not each grammatical part, like its subject, verb, predicate, or complement; but each geographical part: its beginning, middle, and end. Efficient sentences become more persuasive when you put their words in the region of the sentence where they belong. Let's consider each of these three regions. And let's begin at the end, for in trying to make your sentences more persuasive, that is where you should focus your attention first.

A. The End of the Sentence

The end of the sentence is where the reader, no matter how quickly he is reading, pauses. It is thus the region where the point of the sentence, whatever it is, starts to sink in. From this insight emerges the most important principle of sentence construction for lawyers: put the most important *idea*—the most important word or group of words—at the end. In oral advocacy, the most important idea can appear elsewhere, but in written advocacy, it should go at the end because the page does not allow you to indicate (except crudely, perhaps, through italics) the changes in volume and inflection that you would make if you were speaking in court. This advice is common,[1] but lawyers do not appreciate it enough.[2] Failing to put the most important idea at the end of a sentence is perhaps, of all the errors in professional writing, the most pervasive.[3]

To see how putting the most important idea in a sentence at the end makes it more persuasive, consider this sentence in a submission urging an agency not to bring charges against a trader, Jones:

> *It has been five years since the agency completed its investigation and failed to identify any improper trading by Jones, while admonishing four other traders.*

If you are representing Jones, the important idea is that your client is innocent. Revise the sentence to get that idea to the end:

---

1. *See, e.g.*, WILLIAM STRUNK, JR. & E.B. WHITE, THE ELEMENTS OF STYLE 32 (Pearson 4th ed. 2000) ("22. Place the emphatic words of a sentence at the end."); JOSEPH M. WILLIAMS, STYLE: TEN LESSONS IN CLARITY AND GRACE 67 (Scott, Foresman 3d ed. 1989) ("Move the most important information to the end of the sentence."); authorities collected in BRYAN A. GARNER, THE WINNING BRIEF: 100 TIPS FOR PERSUASIVE BRIEFING IN TRIAL AND APPELLATE COURTS 204–07 (Oxford Univ. Press 3d ed. 2014) ("Tip 36: To write forcefully, end your sentences with punch."); RYAN MCCARL, ELEGANT LEGAL WRITING 67–68 (Univ. of California Press 2024).

2. BRYAN A. GARNER, LEGAL WRITING IN PLAIN ENGLISH: A TEXT WITH EXERCISES 59 (Univ. of Chicago Press 3d ed. 2023) ("Here's a principle that many people don't know: the most powerful part of a sentence—the punch position—is the end.").

3. George Gopen, *The Importance of Stress: Indicating the Most Important Word in a Sentence*, 38 LITIGATION, no. 1, Fall 2011, at 20–21 ("Locating the stress-worthy information of a sentence elsewhere than in a stress position is the single most widespread and crippling problem in professional English writing today.").

> *It has been five years since the agency completed its investigation and, while admonishing four other traders,* ***failed to identify any improper trading by Jones****.*

With this small revision, your client is far better served.

Or consider this sentence from the same submission:

> *Jones differed from other traders in that it was not his responsibility to trade stocks on the floor.*

The important idea here is not the location of the trading '*on the floor*.' The important idea here is '*not his responsibility*,' the basis of the distinction the sentence draws. Revise the sentence to:

> *Jones differed from other traders in that trading stocks on the floor was* ***not his responsibility****.*

By putting the most important idea at the end of the sentence, you signal that that is the idea you want to sink in. Knowing this, the judge is more likely to think about it and, in turn, more likely to come to share your view.

Finally, consider the following sentence from the same submission:

> *In fact, Smith testified that 75 to 80 percent of the time, he, not Jones, was trading the stocks at Jones's panel.*

For this mistaken identity defense, the most important idea is the actual identity of the person whose actions have been falsely attributed to your client, Jones. Revise the sentence to:

> *In fact, Smith testified that 75 to 80 percent of the time, the trader trading the stocks at Jones's panel was not Jones but* ***Smith himself****.*

Most readers will find the placement of the true culprit's name here more forceful.

1. Identifying the Most Important Idea

The hardest part of putting the most important idea at the end of the sentence is figuring out which idea is in fact the most important. Consider the following sentence:

> *On May 1, 2021, a grand jury indicted the defendant.*

What is the most important idea in this sentence? It depends on what you are trying to do.

If you are introducing the defendant for the first time in, say, a statement of facts, then the most important idea is the '*defendant*,' and the sentence is good as written.

But what if you are arguing that the limitations period has lapsed? Then the most important idea is '*May 1, 2021*,' and the sentence should be revised to:

> *A grand jury indicted the defendant on May 1, 2021.*

Or what if you are about to argue that the indictment should be dismissed because fewer than 12 jurors voted to indict? If that is the point toward which the passage is building, then the important idea is '*a grand jury*,' and the sentence should be revised to:

> *On May 1, 2021, the defendant was indicted by a grand jury.*

To be followed, perhaps, with:

> *That grand jury on that day lacked a quorum: only 11 jurors were present.*

When trying to find the most important idea in a sentence, ask yourself some questions. In many instances, their answers will direct you to the words you should put at the end.

What implicit question does the sentence answer?

Consider these two sentences:

> *The appellee filed a petition for rehearing on May 15, 2022. The court issued a revised opinion after the appellee filed the petition.*

The implicit question the first sentence answers is: *What did the appellee do?* The answer is: *He filed a petition for rehearing.* So move that idea to the end of the first sentence:

> *On May 15, 2022, the appellee* ***filed a petition for rehearing****. The court issued a revised opinion after the appellee filed the petition.*

Now turn to the second sentence. Its implicit question is: *What did the court then do?* The answer: *The court issued a revised opinion.* So move that idea to the end of the second sentence:

> *On May 15, 2022, the appellee filed a petition for rehearing. After the appellee filed the petition, the court* ***issued a revised opinion****.*

These revised sentences will strike most readers as better merely because the ideas they seek to emphasize appear at the end of each.

For a more argumentative example, consider the second of the following two sentences, which could typically appear at the beginning of a paragraph in the argument section of an opposition or reply brief:

> *The infringer relies upon the Silverman article and the '729 Patent to argue that the asserted claims are obvious.* ***With respect to Claim 10, the infringer faces a complete failure of proof in showing unpatentability over the Silverman article and the '729 Patent.***

The second sentence is inefficient for several reasons: its patent-law jargon; the tic '*with respect to*'; the repetition of the names of the references; the substitution of nominalizations (*failure of proof, unpatentability*) for verbs (*fail, prove*) and adjectives (*unpatentable, obvious*). All these faults can be corrected:

> *The infringer relies upon the Silverman article and the '729 Patent to argue that the asserted claims are obvious.* ***The infringer's argument fails completely because he cannot prove that these references render Claim 10 obvious.***

But even so, the sentence is not quite as persuasive as it might be. The reason is that the answer to the sentence's implicit question—*Should the infringer's argument about Claim 10 succeed?*—does not appear at the end. Move the answer—*No, it should fail.*—there:

> *The infringer relies upon the Silverman article and the '729 Patent to argue that the asserted claims are obvious. Because the infringer cannot prove by clear and convincing evidence that these references render Claim 10 obvious,* ***his argument fails****.*

The revision also substitutes the legally applicable standard of proof—'*by clear and convincing evidence*'—for the bombastic '*complete failure*' or '*fails completely*.' As discussed later in this chapter, eliminating bombast also makes sentences more persuasive.

What words describe the basis for a distinction?

A major tool of argument is drawing distinctions: between cases, between fact patterns, between results under different interpretations of laws, etc. For these distinctions to get the oxygen they need, their bases should appear at the end of the sentence.

Here is a sentence considered in the preceding chapter:

> *This automatic email-deletion policy will result in the loss of not only harmful evidence but also potentially helpful evidence.*

This sentence argues against an automatic deletion policy by observing that the policy fails to distinguish between deletion of harmful and helpful evidence. The sentence is written fairly well, as it delays to the end of the sentence the result that is most likely to dissuade the client from adopting the policy: '*the loss of potentially helpful evidence*.' But it can be even better. The distinction the sentence draws is between '*harmful*' and '*helpful*.' Accordingly, the force of the distinction becomes even greater if you move one of those words to the end. You can do that easily:

> *This automatic email-deletion policy will result in the loss of not only harmful evidence but also evidence that is potentially* ***helpful***.

This sentence is equally efficient but marginally more persuasive because the practical defect of the policy—the loss of evidence that is *helpful*—is somewhat clearer.

What words introduce new information or a new concept?

Many sentences introduce a piece of new information or a new concept. In such sentences, it's nearly always a good idea to put that new idea at the end. This is a core technique of textbook and other instructional writing. Although legal writing is primarily persuasive, significant parts of legal arguments and the entirety of background statements (see Chapter 9, Background Statements) teach judges things they need to know. Putting the most important idea—*i.e.*, the new idea—at the end serves that goal.

Here is a paragraph from the beginning of a statement of facts that illustrates this advice. The new idea in each sentence (in bold) appears at the beginning of each sentence:

> ***The patent for the drug obviramate*** *is the subject of this case.* ***To prevent heart attacks, strokes and other atherothrombotic conditions****, physicians prescribe obviramate.* ***Patients who have received stents*** *are also prescribed obviramate.*

Here is a revision that places the new idea of each sentence at the end of each:

> *This case concerns the* ***patent for the drug obviramate****. Obviramate is prescribed* ***to prevent heart attacks, strokes and other atherothrombotic conditions****. Obviramate is also prescribed to* ***patients who have received stents****.*

In the revision, the reader encounters the new information at the end of every sentence. She thus can process the new information with the help of the pause that a period provides.

Consider whether the new information in this sentence appears at the end:

> *National security information should be classified as* CONFIDENTIAL *if the unauthorized disclosure of that information could reasonably be expected to damage the national security interests of the United States.*

In fact, you cannot identify the new information in this sentence by just reading its words in isolation. Depending on the information that preceded the sentence, either the nomenclature 'CONFIDENTIAL' or the meaning of that nomenclature ('*if the unauthorized disclosure . . .*') may be the new idea the writer is trying to convey. And yet, there is a clue: the writer placed 'CONFIDENTIAL' in all caps. That typographical emphasis indicates that the primary goal of this sentence is to introduce unfamiliar nomenclature. If so, 'CONFIDENTIAL' should appear at the end:

> *If the unauthorized disclosure of National Security Information could reasonably be expected to damage the national security interests of the United States, the information should be classified as "Confidential."*

By putting the new idea warranting emphasis at the end of the sentence, the writer no longer needs to clumsily resort to all caps to convey that emphasis.

Indeed, perhaps the surest way to identify the most important idea in a sentence is to find the word that you would emphasize typographically (through italics or boldface type) if you were so inclined—or perhaps that you have already so highlighted in your draft:

> *Petition 446 improperly delegates authority to determine the amount of the yearly increase in the state minimum wage to the* ***federal*** *Department of Labor.*

becomes:

> *Petition 446 improperly delegates authority to determine the amount of the yearly increase in the state minimum wage to the Department of Labor, an arm of the* ***federal government****.*

The second version is superior because the basis for the distinction the sentence is drawing—delegation to a federal department rather than to a state—appears at the end. For the same reason:

> *Today, there are* ***more*** *ways to challenge patent validity than when Westinghouse was decided in 1871.*

should become:

> *As compared with 1871, when Westinghouse was decided, the number of ways to challenge patent validity today is* ***greater****.*

The basis for the distinction is numerosity.

2. Moving Words to the End

Once you identify the most important idea in a sentence, getting that idea to the end is usually easy. To be sure, word order is more rigid in English than in many other languages. Unlike readers of, say, Classical Greek or Russian, English readers like to see a grammatical subject relatively early in a clause or sentence to avoid getting confused. But several features of English make this constraint less of a straitjacket than it might seem. Here are simple techniques for pushing every significant type of word to the end of a sentence.

✦ **Objects**

In most basic English sentences, objects appear at the end. So if the most important idea in a sentence is an object, it will tend to show up there naturally:

> *On May 15, 2022, the appellee filed* ***a petition for rehearing****. (Direct Object)*
>
> *On May 1, 2021, a grand jury indicted* ***the defendant****. (Direct Object)*
>
> *The court should order the defendant to transfer the funds to* ***the escrow agent****. (Indirect Object)*
>
> *The court distinguished this case from* ***the other****. (Prepositional Object)*
>
> *The grand jury indicted the defendant on* ***May 1, 2021****. (Prepositional Object)*

But objects warranting emphasis can move away from their natural terminal position as sentences start to get more complex. If the most important idea in this sentence:

> *The grand jury did not indict the defendant until* ***May 1, 2021****, even though he was arrested on February 1.*

is the date of the indictment, then don't let the clause about the date of arrest block the exit. Revise to:

> *Even though the defendant was arrested on February 1, 2021, the grand jury did not indict him until* ***May 1****.*

If you can't extricate less important words or phrases from the end of a sentence, consider breaking the sentence up into two:

> *The grand jury did not indict the defendant until May 1, 2021, upon which he retained counsel.*

becomes:

> *The grand jury did not indict the defendant until May 1, 2021. On that day, he retained counsel.*

✦ Subjects

If the most important idea in a sentence is its grammatical subject, it's easy to relocate it to the end of the sentence. It is easy even though English generally requires subjects to precede verbs. Just convert the voice of the verb from active to passive.

> *The Supreme Court reversed the decision.*

becomes:

> *The decision was reversed by the Supreme Court.*

Changing the voice of a verb from active to passive, by definition, makes the verb's subject an object. Thus, because objects most naturally appear after verbs, recasting a verb in the passive voice automatically pushes the verb's subject to the terminal region of the sentence.

Of course, writing texts frown upon the passive voice. The reason is that in many sentences, using an actively voiced verb will make the sentence more forthright. And yet, as all the good texts also appreciate, the passive voice can be a very useful tool. As in the simple example from the last paragraph, it allows you to move the grammatical subject to the end of the sentence, where the subject can get the emphasis it deserves.

Another useful feature of the passive voice is that it may allow you to hide the subject altogether. In some settings, that can be the right move. If you are the plaintiff's counsel, you will want to revise this sentence:

> *Because Plaintiff's counsel mistook the deadline for substantial completion of document production, Plaintiff failed to produce the documents in a timely fashion.*

to:

> *Owing to a mistake about the deadline for substantial completion of document production, the documents were not produced in a timely fashion.*

Here, one of the things that makes the passive voice the enemy of many writing teachers—that it suppresses the identity of the true actor—is the very thing that makes it useful.

Sometimes identifying the subject, though not disadvantageous, will not serve any purpose. For example:

> *The FDA promulgated the regulation in 2014 pursuant to authority the agency received through the XYZ Act.*

is a good, actively voiced sentence. But you may prefer to put the spotlight of the sentence on the regulation, not the FDA, if the judge already knows that the FDA is the promulgating agency or if that detail is not important. The passive voice will allow you to cast the regulation in the starring role:

> *The regulation was promulgated in 2014 pursuant to authority the FDA received through the XYZ Act.*

Note, however, that once you have substituted a passively voiced verb for an active, you can often improve the sentence further by finding an actively voiced verb that is the exact equivalent:

> *The regulation issued in 2014 pursuant to authority the FDA received through the XYZ Act.*

Some readers may prefer the actively voiced '*issued*' for the passively voiced '*was promulgated*' because the active voice makes the sentence a bit more direct.

In sum, the passive voice, for all the criticism it receives, is nonetheless a valuable tool for moving the grammatical subject to the end of a sentence or, alternatively, for de-emphasizing it. No writer should want to avoid the passive voice altogether. The active voice should be your default, but you should not hesitate to shift to the passive voice when you have a good reason.

✦ Verbs

It's sometimes hard to move a verb to the end of a sentence, especially if the verb requires an object or prepositional phrase. Nonetheless, if the most important idea in a sentence is such a verb, you can often find a way to get it there. The most useful technique is to make the verb into a noun. Although nominalized verbs can often make sentences inefficient (see Chapter 2, The Efficient Sentence, at pp. 25–26), nominalizing a verb will sometimes allow it to stand at the end of a sentence, where it will receive proper emphasis. If so, that is a good reason to use the nominalization. Consider the following sentence:

> *To obtain post-petition financing, a Chapter 11 debtor must file a motion, and the court must approve the financing.*

This sentence is okay, but the idea the writer wants to emphasize is that financing will not be obtained unless it is *approved*. For that, nominalization, with a few harmonizing changes, comes to the writer's aid:

> *To obtain post-petition financing, a Chapter 11 debtor must file a motion and secure the court's* ***approval****.*

✦ Adjectives

Even adjectives, which tend to directly precede the noun they describe, can be dispatched to the end of a sentence. Recall this pair of examples from a few pages ago:

> *This automatic email-deletion policy will result in the loss of not only harmful evidence but also potentially* ***helpful*** *evidence.*

> *This automatic email-deletion policy will result in the loss of not only harmful evidence but also evidence that is potentially* ***helpful****.*

In the second sentence, '*helpful*' has become a *predicate adjective*: it operates as if it were a noun—here, the object of '*is*.' The conversion allows the adjective to appear as the last word of the sentence even though adjectives generally precede nouns. Granted, the conversion also increases slightly the word count of the sentence, but it does not violate the rule to eliminate unnecessary words. Words that make a sentence more persuasive are necessary.

Under some circumstances, you can move an adjective to the end of a sentence by nominalizing it:

> *This automatic email-deletion policy will result in the loss of not only harmful evidence but also evidence of potential* ***help****.*

In this revision, the original adjective, '*helpful*,' has become the noun '*help*.' But nominalizing adjectives, as in this revision, tends to be less effective than nominalizing verbs. Consider the following sentence:

> *The court issued a sound decision.*

Here, the important idea is the adjective, '*sound*.' But nominalizing it to get it to the end:

> *The court issued a decision of* ***sound****ness.*

makes the short sentence clumsy, bureaucratic, even pompous. Most readers would probably prefer a predicate adjective:

> *The court issued a decision that is* ***sound****.*

Or better, if the context permits:

> *The court's decision is* ***sound****.*

✦ Adverbs

Even though adverbs most efficiently appear immediately before or after the verb they describe, this placement is not essential. If the adverb conveys the idea you are trying to emphasize, you can sometimes place it relatively far from the verb it describes:

> *The Supreme Court* ***reversed*** *the Federal Circuit's decision* ***unanimously****.*

But, as noted in the last chapter, an adverb can tolerate only so much separation. In the following extreme version of an earlier example, putting '*unanimously*' at the end of the sentence makes the sentence incomprehensible:

> *The Supreme Court* ***reversed*** *the Federal Circuit's decision holding Section 264 of the America Invents Act unconstitutional* ***unanimously****.*

But that does not mean that '*unanimously*' needs to be buried in the middle of the sentence. Use the passive voice to move the verb closer to the end, where it will allow the terminal adverb to function properly:

> *The Federal Circuit's decision holding Section 264 of the America Invents Act unconstitutional* ***was reversed*** *by the Supreme Court* ***unanimously****.*

Here, the passive voice also lets you shorten the sentence by suppressing its original subject, '*the Supreme Court*':

> *The Federal Circuit's decision holding Section 264 of the America Invents Act unconstitutional* ***was reversed unanimously****.*

Sometimes that may make the sentence more efficient.

B. The Beginning of the Sentence

While you use the end of the sentence to persuade, you use the beginning to prepare the ground for that effort.

1. Topic Identification

The beginning of the sentence alerts the reader to the topic of the sentence and, in so doing, can help keep the focus of a paragraph steady. Consider the following short example from a few pages ago:

> *This case concerns the patent for the drug obviramate. Obviramate is prescribed to prevent heart attacks, strokes and other atherothrombotic conditions. Obviramate is also prescribed to patients who have received stents.*

The appearance of '*obviramate*' at the beginning of the last two sentences signals that the grammatical subject of each sentence is also its topic. Writers determined to avoid the passive voice will revise the paragraph to:

> *This case concerns the patent for the drug obviramate. Physicians prescribe obviramate to prevent heart attacks, strokes and other atherothrombotic conditions. Physicians also prescribe obviramate to patients who have received stents.*

But the revision has not improved the passage. To the contrary, by turning the reader's focus to the prescriber rather than the prescribed, the revision has created a false impression that the focus will now shift to prescribing practice rather than stay on the drug itself. As paragraphs get more complex, too many shifts in focus will make the reader carsick.

2. Sentence Connection

You also use the beginning of a sentence to help the judge understand how that sentence relates to the previous sentence. Armed with that understanding, the judge will be more receptive to the argument the sentence or paragraph is trying to make.

✦ Lookback

Let's return, for example, to the sentence:

> *On May 14, 2021, the defendant was indicted by a grand jury.*

How should you begin the next sentence in a motion arguing that the grand jury issued its indictment without a quorum? By echoing the preceding sentence's two final words, '*grand jury*':

> *That* ***grand jury*** *on that day lacked a quorum: only 11 jurors were present.*

By beginning with the same words, '*grand jury*,' that concluded the preceding sentence, this second sentence allows the judge to see the connection between what he just read and what he is reading now.

The potential value of repeating at the beginning of a sentence the word(s) that concluded the preceding is not novel or unique to English. In his second-century textbook on rhetoric (the closest classical analogue to legal writing), Hermogenes of Tarsus called the technique *epanastrophe*, literally, *return*.[4] For English speakers, *look-back* might be a better metaphor.

To move words to the beginning of a sentence, you can use some of the same techniques English offers for moving a word to the end. Just as the passive voice can move the subject of an actively voiced verb to the end of a sentence, so too it can move that verb's object to the beginning:

---

4. HERMOGENES' ON TYPES OF STYLE 59–60 (Cecil Wooten trans., Univ. of North Carolina Press 1987).

> *On October 2, 2022, the parties executed a book contract that called for quarterly royalty payments. The payments were capped at 10% of the net sales revenue the publisher realized.*

Placing '*cap*' in the passive voice allows you to begin the second sentence with the noun, '*payments*,' where it echoes the same word at the end of the first. The repetition also suggests to the judge that he should start to focus his attention on royalty payments rather than other aspects of the contract's performance. If that is in fact where he should focus his attention, the reference to those payments at the beginning of the sentence is apt.

Lookback will often help you begin a sentence, but it is not always necessary or practical. And using it too much can become tedious or seem contrived. If you want to draw a connection between two sentences in a more subtle way, other techniques are available.

✦ Phrases and Subordinate Clauses

You can, for example, begin a sentence with a participial phrase, a prepositional phrase, or a subordinate clause that embeds within it the idea with which the prior sentence concluded:

> **Participial Phrase:** *In B v. D, the Supreme Court* ***held that [. . .]. Applying that holding****, this court should . . .*
>
> **Prepositional Phrase:** *The Supreme Court construed the 1984 Bail Reform Act in* ***B v. D. In that case****, the defendant assaulted a federal marshal while the defendant was drunk.*
>
> **Subordinate Clause:** *In B v. D, the defendant was detained because the court found clear and convincing evidence that his appearance at trial could not be ensured by any combination of* ***conditions. Although the opinion in that case did not consider whether electronic monitoring was a suitable pre-release condition****, the court's reasoning implied that it would have reached the same conclusion even if that mode of pretrial monitoring had been available.*

In the second sentence of each of these passages, the writer has led off with the idea from the end of the first sentence but has not used the same words:

held that: Applying that holding

B v. D: In that case

conditions: Although the opinion . . . condition

In this way, the writer shows the reader the connection between the two sentences without concluding and beginning the sentences identically.

✦ Logical Traffic Signals

English offers many prefatory words, conjunctions, or phrases (*but, therefore, by contrast*, etc.) to show the logical connection between sentences. These connecting words or phrases, when placed at or very near the beginning of a sentence, can be analogized to traffic signals or road signs: they show the reader the direction in which the argument is heading or turning. Successful fiction writers use logical traffic signals only occasionally. You will find them only rarely in the works of a novelist whose works people read voluntarily. But that doesn't mean you should eschew them. Despite their non-colloquial, even pedantic tone, logical traffic signals help you guide a judge through the logic of complex legal arguments, a difficult task fiction writers do not face. You should not feel awkward using them, at least not in the argument sections of briefs. No brief can function without them.

Sometimes lawyers get in the habit of using some logical traffic signals too often (*e.g., indeed, moreover, however, thus*) when others might serve equally well. To fight that tendency, here is a small thesaurus of the most common logical traffic signals, organized according to the function they serve:

To Add:

Additionally,
Also,
And

By the same token,
Further,
In addition,
In the same vein,
Moreover,
Nor
Relatedly,
What is more,

To Show Cause and Result:

Accordingly,
As a result,
Consequently,
Consistently with this [approach, theory, argument],
Hence,
Therefore,
Thus,

To Contrast:

But
Conversely,
. . . , *however,*
In/by contrast,
Nevertheless,
Nonetheless,
On the contrary,
On the other hand, . . . (if preceded by '*On the one hand,*')

To Clarify:

In effect,
In other words,
Put differently/another way,
Simply put,
That is,

To Dismiss or Discount:

Be that as it may,
Either way,
In any event,
Nevertheless,
Nonetheless,

To Illustrate:

For example,
For instance,
In particular,
[More] specifically,

To Emphasize:

A fortiori,
Again,
Importantly,
Indeed,
In fact,
More important,
Notably,
Surely,

To Analogize or Compare:

By analogy,
By extension,
Here,
In like manner,
In the same way,
Likewise,
Relatedly,
Similarly,
So too here,

To Qualify or Concede:

Certainly,

Granted,

No doubt,

Of course,

That said,

To be sure,

True,

Yes,

To Argue Alternatively:

Alternatively,

In the alternative,

To Conclude:

Finally,

For all these reasons,

In conclusion,

In brief,

In sum,

Lastly,

To conclude,

3. Ordinals and Their Overuse

Many lawyers love to lead off sentences with ordinal numbers, often emphasizing them with italics: *First, Second, Third,* . . . The following paragraph from the beginning of an argument is typical:

> *Plaintiff's claim fails for three reasons. First, Plaintiff lacks standing to raise the claim. Second, the claim is time-barred. Third, Plaintiff did not suffer any compensable damages.*

Lawyers who use these a lot believe that the succession of ordinals enhances the flow of the paragraph and gives the judge a helpful overview of the arguments that will unfold.

Really?

Granted, the featured paragraph benefits from the ordinals; omitting them would make it choppy:

> *Plaintiff's claim fails for three reasons. Plaintiff lacks standing to raise the claim. The claim is time-barred. Plaintiff did not suffer any compensable damages.*

But are the ordinals in the original example doing what the words at the beginning of a sentence are supposed to do?

They are not identifying the topic of a sentence or a paragraph, major roles words at the beginning of a sentence should play. To the contrary, in the preceding example, the ordinals jarringly arrest the judge's attention. They focus it on a circumstance—the sequence of the ensuing arguments—that is not interesting or important.

Nor do ordinals effectively perform the second role words at the beginning of a sentence play: showing the connection between the ensuing sentence and the preceding. All they do is communicate that the lawyer has several arguments and that the first argument appears first; the second, second; the third, third, etc. Their content is close to nil.

Far better is to revise the paragraph in a way that allows you to use the opening words of the sentences to show the relations and differences between each of the previewed arguments. Although this can sometimes take some thought, that thought is almost always worthwhile. It forces you to think more about your several arguments and why you are in fact sequencing them as you are:

> *Plaintiff's claim fails for three reasons: constitutional, procedural and substantive. As a matter of constitutional law, plaintiff lacks standing to raise the claim. Moreover, the claim is procedurally flawed because it is time-barred. And even if Plaintiff had standing to assert the claim in a timely manner, the claim would still fail because Plaintiff did not suffer any compensable damages.*

In place of a firing line of content-less ordinal adjectives, the opening words of the second, third, and fourth sentences describe attributes of the arguments that will help the judge remember and evaluate them. The revised beginnings of each sentence will also give the judge a sense whether he may usefully consider them in an order other than the one the lawyer has presented. For example, the opening of the final sentence ("*And even if . . .*") signals to the judge that the lawyer considers the last argument an argument-in-the-alternative, to which the judge may turn first if he thinks that might be a better use of his time.

There may well be contexts in which it is helpful to emphasize the numerical order in which arguments or reasons are presented. But as a general matter, ordinals show up at the beginnings of sentences far too often. The reasons are several. Some lawyers put ordinals at the beginning because they were taught in school that they effectively organize essays. Some lawyers put them there because all their peers do. Worst of all, some lawyers put them there because they are too intellectually lazy to think through the relations between their arguments and to build into their paragraphs logical traffic signals and other things that make those relations clear. None of these reasons is strong. In beginning sentences, avoid ordinals as much as you can. Reserve the beginning for words that can better help the judge see how the rest of the sentence is going to unfold.

C. The Middle of the Sentence

And what about the middle of the sentence? What words go there? The flippant answer is: *Anything that doesn't go anywhere else.* That isn't all that far from the truth. The middle of the sentence is where you put all the words you need to make the beginning and end of the sentence work. More helpfully, you should conceive of the middle of the sentence as the region that transports the reader as efficiently as possible to the end of the sentence, where persuasion—your overarching goal—occurs. For this task, the efficiency-enhancing rules and principles discussed in the prior chapter are all you need.

Consider, however, some words that should not go in the middle of the sentence or, indeed, anywhere else. Among those are words that convey bombast or sarcasm.

The reason to avoid bombast requires little discussion. All lawyers know how satisfying it is to declaim that an adversary's argument is *fatally flawed*, *absurd*, *disingenuous*, or *preposterous*, or to make *ad hominem* attacks on the adversary's integrity. Most experienced lawyers have also encountered co-counsel or clients who, after receiving a first draft of a brief too restrained for their taste, send over a heavy markup larded with over-the-top expressions of outrage. After innumerable bar association and judicial conferences at which judges have lamented how they find such hyperbole distracting and wearisome, lawyers should take the hint. You should refrain from rebutting arguments—including the many that are truly preposterous and absurd—with chest-beating and disparagement. Let the analytical force of your arguments make their absurdity clear.

Sarcasm also has no place in any sentence, but it calls for a more nuanced discussion. Anyone who follows television or internet political commentators knows that human beings enjoy watching articulate people advocate extreme positions sarcastically. The taste for sarcasm is so strong that prime-time pundits who make their nightly sermons drip—no, gush—with sarcasm find themselves better compensated than even the most successful trial lawyers. Many politicians on both sides of the spectrum also use sarcasm to devastating effect, especially at staged political rallies. But note that in these contexts, sarcasm is deployed solely to entertain and to firm up support for a position among groups of like-minded people. It is not used to flip votes or to persuade a person whose mind is not made up—or, worse, a person who has formed an initial view opposed to one's own. For the undecided or hostile reader—the reader for whom lawyers are retained to write—sarcasm is off-putting, even threatening. It will harden confirmation biases more reliably than any other rhetorical device. For this reason, you should purge sarcasm from all your submissions. Unless the judge is already on your side (in which case the submission likely does not matter), sarcasm carries risks the prudent lawyer should not take.

* * *

Knowing which words to put at the beginning, in the middle, and, especially, at the end of a sentence is the surest path to making a sentence as persuasive as it can be. The most important idea—the idea you want to sink in—should go at the end, as it generally can. Once you have put the most important idea at the end, use the beginning of the sentence to fix or sharpen the focal point and to show the sentence's relation to the preceding sentence. By doing these things—and not letting any sarcasm or bombast slip in—you can be sure that if the sentence fails to persuade, the reason will probably not be bad drafting.

CHAPTER 4

The Professional Sentence

The third attribute of a good legal sentence is that it is professional: that it strikes an educated, experienced member of the legal profession as having been written by someone similar. This book takes up professionalism last in this set of chapters about the sentence because, of the three attributes of a good sentence, professionalism is the least important. If, using the tips and guidance of the last two chapters, you can write sentences that are efficient and persuasive, you have mastered the most important aspects of drafting sentences, and you are well on your way to becoming an excellent legal writer.

Professionalism is nonetheless important. It could even be considered a component of persuasiveness, the most important attribute of all. Here is why. The most important source of persuasive power is credibility. Credibility comes in substantial part from building a track record with the reader for honesty. You do that above all by never making a statement that is not 100 percent true. But before you build your track record for honesty (or if you have undermined it in some way), credibility comes from impressing the reader as someone knowledgeable. If the reader is a judge, it means impressing the judge as a well-educated person who has learned law deeply and broadly with the intelligence that effort requires. That is the hallmark of a professional.

At minimum, a professional sentence follows conventions of English spelling and grammar, but this book will not consider these subjects. In truth, spelling mistakes in briefs are fairly rare these days, undoubtedly because of spell-checking software. The few mistakes that find their way into briefs are generally homonyms (principle–principal; affect–effect; defendants'–defendants). Basic grammatical mistakes are also relatively rare, perhaps surprisingly since most lawyers today attended schools and colleges that, for the most part, abandoned rigorous instruction in grammar in the 1960s. The scarcity of such mistakes may stem from the prevalence of grammar-checking software. But despite the increasing power of this software, all lawyers, no matter what their level of education or experience, should at some point read a short text that covers points of English grammar most relevant to proficient English speakers.[1] The experience will almost certainly teach you something useful that you did not know.

In practice, sentences come off as unprofessional mostly because they fail to adhere to norms of professional diction. Faulty diction appears most often when words are used with their correct individual meanings but in combinations that strike the experienced reader as being somehow off. Here are two examples:

The witness alleged that he saw the accident.

The witness claimed that he saw the accident.

The sentences are fine as a matter of everyday English, but when you are writing for judges, they need tweaks. A litigator and judge will appreciate that witnesses *testify to*, *state*, or, when subscribing to a sworn statement, *declare* facts. Only parties to lawsuits *allege* facts and then only when they are submitting pleadings. Only parties to lawsuits make *claims*, and when they do so, the statements pertain to legal causes of action (*e.g.*, trespass, breach of contract), not to underlying facts. Again, the correct verbs for underlying facts are *testify*, *state*, *assert*, or *declare*.

In a similar vein, the diction of the following sentence is not professional:

The expert stated that the patent was invalid.

This sentence is slightly off because under the rules of evidence, experts do not state or testify to facts or legal conclusions. They assume facts, preferably those in the record, and then offer opinions. An expert who is doing anything other than opining and stating assumed facts or bases for her opinions is, according to evidence law, not functioning as an expert. The better, more professional verb here is *opined*.

---

1. *E.g.*, *Rules of English: Understanding Grammar*, *in* New Oxford American Dictionary 1962–85 (Oxford Univ. Press 2d ed. 2005).

It is impossible to catalog every permutation of words in unprofessional combinations. Nonetheless, this book can offer advice for eliminating them from your speech and writing. The bad news is that following the advice is time-consuming. The good news is that the advice is easy to follow.

The advice begins with appreciating that the diction U.S. litigators use in court is a dialect of English. As a dialect, it is not learned in the same way that math or chemistry is learned. It is not studied or memorized. Rather, it is acquired in the same way that elementary speakers of a foreign language ratchet up their proficiency: by listening, listening, and listening to proficient speakers; by reading, reading, and reading well-written prose. For law students, the process begins in the first law school class when, for the first time in their lives, they hear professors lecturing and asking questions about cases and other legal materials. But it does not end there. It needs to be supplemented. Much of the supplementation comes from reading the many cases assigned in class. From these, you learn not only their holdings but also how proficient writers of Litigation English combine words. You do not read the cases with this conscious purpose in mind. The process occurs naturally and gradually. If you take enough hard-core law classes, that process will greatly expand your proficiency in Litigation English by the time you graduate. You will not realize it, but it will.

For many, law school alone may not offer enough exposure to Litigation English, but it is not hard to increase it. Fortunately, opportunities for increasing your exposure to Litigation English extensively and painlessly are much greater in this century than in earlier. If, in the 20th century, you wanted to immerse yourself in well-spoken Litigation English, you had to go to appellate arguments when the courts were in session and spend hours taking the arguments in. Today, you can spend commuting time or time you spend cooking, exercising, or cleaning your home listening to downloads of Supreme Court and other high-caliber appellate arguments. As a general matter and at least as of this writing, the judges and lawyers participating in those are highly proficient speakers of Litigation English, no matter what you think of their jurisprudence or skill. Many of them will speak Litigation English as if they were native speakers even if they make mistakes when they write it.

Another important way to improve your proficiency in Litigation English is to read supplemental sources voraciously. The best material for this purpose is opinions from cases you find interesting. If you find the cases boring, you will not pay attention to the language they are using, and the exercise will be a waste of time. But if you are interested in a legal subject—any subject—then get a pile of appellate opinions on that subject and start reading them whenever you have a free moment. A more bite-size source of Litigation English is the syllabi prepared by the Reporter of the U.S. Supreme Court. These summaries of opinions are short and informative, and they have long defined proper Litigation English diction in a way that BBC announcers once defined the proper pronunciation of U.K. English.

This process of immersion will not work unless you do it a lot over a long period of time. But if you do it—do not work too hard at it; just listen and read; do not force yourself to follow the arguments in detail—you will acquire proficiency in Litigation English. Your career in legal writing and oral advocacy will go more smoothly for having invested time in this totally passive activity.

To offer a more active approach, this book will classify the most common errors in diction so that you may get better at spotting them. The three most common classes involve mismatched words:

- subjects and verbs;
- verbs and objects;
- verbs (or a derived nominalization) and prepositions.

Here is a sentence that exemplifies all three classes of errors:

> *Our constitutional system starts with the premise that, absent the narrowest of possible exceptions, the federal government cannot consign its citizens to unconstitutional procedures.*

> **Subject–Verb Mismatch:** In this sentence, the pairing of the subject, '*Our constitutional system*,' with the verb, '*start*,' is awkward because a *system* does not *start* with a premise. It *arises* from or out of a circumstance or is *based* on something.

> **Verb–Preposition Mismatch:** In this sentence, the pairing of the verb '*starts*' with the preposition '*with*' is also problematic, because even things that start do not start *with* premises; they start *from* premises.
>
> **Verb–Object Mismatch:** Finally, the pairing of the verb '*consign*' with the object '*procedures*' is awkward because people or things are generally consigned to inferior statuses or conditions, not to *procedures*. Better verb–object pairings would have been '*subject its citizens*' or '*require its citizens to follow*.'

With all three errors in diction corrected, the sentence reads:

> *Our constitutional system is based upon the premise that, absent the narrowest of possible exceptions, the federal government cannot require its citizens to follow unconstitutional procedures.*

Other revisions are warranted, but they will take us back to subjects already covered.

The foregoing example (from a brief filed in the Supreme Court by an eminent lawyer who had once served as the U.S. Solicitor General) presents a notable combination of flaws in diction. But examples of similar errors can easily be found in the majority of briefs filed in any state supreme court or the Supreme Court. The prevalence of unprofessional diction in briefs filed even at such a high level of the court system and by elite practitioners shows that the problem warrants attention. Even if a judge does not mind the malapropisms, they will, like slightly faulty reading glasses, make a brief seem less focused than it might otherwise be.

Here, drawn from a random selection of briefs recently filed in the highest courts of the United States, are examples of mismatched words falling into each of the three categories just described. Even if you find some of the proposed revisions unduly pedantic (and perhaps some are), consider that at least some judges will find the original diction to be an irritant. To stay on topic, the proposed revisions will focus only on improving diction and not on enhancing efficiency or persuasiveness with the techniques described in the last two chapters.

✦ Subject–Verb Mismatch

> *To the contrary, the Act promises to grant judicial review over a specified set of claims.*

An act cannot *promise* anything. Revise to:

> *To the contrary, the Act provides for judicial review over a specified set of claims.*

* * *

> *Although the Grain Warehouse Act instructs that it is to be interpreted liberally in favor of claimants, this instruction does not eliminate the specific requirements set out by the General Assembly.*

An act also cannot *instruct* anything. Revise to:

> *Although the Grain Warehouse Act states that it is to be interpreted liberally in favor of claimants, this statement does not eliminate the specific requirements set out by the General Assembly.*

* * *

> *Judge Johnson usurped his authority when he vacated the plea to the charge of menacing.*

Usurp takes an object that someone else holds and that the usurper has wrongfully arrogated. Revise to:

> *Judge Johnson exceeded his authority when he vacated the plea to the charge of menacing.*

* * *

> *Such diluted conceptions of good faith stifle the progress of science, whose lifeblood depends on dissent and outlier opinions.*

Lifeblood does not *depend* on things. Revise to:

> *Such diluted conceptions of good faith stifle the progress of science, whose lifeblood is dissent and outlier opinions.*

* * *

> *Even assuming that Locke entails that strict scrutiny should not apply here, rational basis review is not the appropriate substitute.*

Cases do not *entail* propositions. Revise to:

> *Even assuming that Locke dictates that strict scrutiny should not apply here, rational basis review is not the appropriate substitute.*

* * *

> *Amicus argues that the common thread uniting the five forms of relief enumerated in subsection (b)(1) is that immigration judges can grant or deny them in removal proceedings.*

Threads do not *unite* things; threads *run through* things or *tie* them together. Revise to:

> *Amicus argues that the common thread running through the five forms of relief enumerated in subsection (b)(1) is that immigration judges can grant or deny them in removal proceedings.*

✦ Verb–Object Mismatch

> *The Court of Appeals's reasoning cannot resurrect the trial court's failure to decide the issue.*

The image of a dead trial court failure, which *resurrect* conjures, is odd. Revise to:

> *The Court of Appeals's reasoning cannot excuse the trial court's failure to decide the issue.*

* * *

> *Each of the five provisions covered by subsection (b)(1) is a form of discretionary immigration relief deploying this traditional two-part structure.*

A form does not *deploy* a structure; it *displays*, *exhibits*, or *has* a structure. Revise to:

> *Each of the five provisions covered by subsection (b)(1) is a form of discretionary immigration relief having this traditional two-part structure.*

* * *

> *The strong presumption in favor of judicial review over agency action fortifies the plain language of subsection (b)(i).*

Statutory *language* is not fortified; *conclusions* are. Revise to:

> *The strong presumption in favor of judicial review over agency action fortifies the conclusion to be drawn from the plain language of subsection (b)(i).*

* * *

> *Distinguishing between discretionary and non-discretionary determinations offers an administrable line for judges to apply.*

Lines are not *offered* or *applied*; they are *drawn*. Revise to:

> *Distinguishing between discretionary and non-discretionary determinations draws a line against which judges can apply an administrable standard.*

* * *

> *The court must also indulge on behalf of the non-moving party every legitimate inference reasonably derived from the record.*

Unlike fallacies or weaknesses, inferences are not *indulged*; they are *drawn*. Revise to:

> *The court must also draw on behalf of the non-moving party every legitimate inference reasonably derived from the record.*

* * *

> *The court ruled that an assignor could argue as a complete defense to infringement that his device practiced prior art described in an expired patent.*

In formal legal writing, defenses are not *argued*; they are *asserted*. Revise to:

> *The court ruled that an assignor could assert as a complete defense to infringement that his device practiced prior art described in an expired patent.*

* * *

The Supremacy Clause likewise does not immunize the President from the everyday obligations of citizenship.

An individual is *immunized* against the adverse effects of something (an illness, a lawsuit) that acts upon him; not from duties the individual must actively perform. Revise to:

The Supremacy Clause likewise does not relieve the President of the everyday obligations of citizenship.

✦ Verb (or Nominalization)–Preposition Mismatch

Each of the Thunder Basin factors points against a finding of implied jurisdiction-stripping.

Something points *to* or *away from* something else, not *against* it. Revise to:

Each of the Thunder Basin factors points away from a finding of implied jurisdiction-stripping.

Or change the verb so that it properly takes the preposition *against*:

Each of the Thunder Basin factors weighs against a finding of implied jurisdiction-stripping.

* * *

For all their disdain toward Respondents, Petitioner and its amici offer no meaningful alternative to their reading of the law.

Disdain is held *for* something, not *toward* it. Revise to:

For all their disdain for Respondents, Petitioner and its amici offer no meaningful alternative to their reading of the law.

* * *

Just as the FHA confers a private cause of action to "any person" who is denied truthful housing information, Title III confers a private cause of action to "any person who is being subjected to discrimination on the basis of disability."

Confer takes the preposition *on* or *upon*, not *to*. Revise to:

Just as the FHA confers a private cause of action on "any person" who is denied truthful housing information, Title III

> *confers a private cause of action on "any person who is being subjected to discrimination on the basis of disability."*

Enough said.

Clichéd Metaphors: In acquiring a professional voice, you can sometimes go too far. Take care not to become so proficient in Litigation English that you describe your adversary's arguments with metaphors so common in briefs that they have become clichés:

> *too thin a reed*
>
> *a sword and a shield*
>
> *fatally flawed*
>
> *a second bite at the apple*
>
> *a red herring*
>
> *smoke and mirrors*
>
> *flip/turn an argument on its head/upside down*

There is nothing wrong with likening arguments to plants, weapons, bodies, fruit, fish, magic-trick paraphernalia, or other physical objects. To the contrary, the foregoing metaphors were surely quite effective, even clever, when first used long ago. But for briefs at least, their depreciation cycle ended long ago. Keep your writing fresh by retiring them.

* * *

Writing good sentences is only the beginning of good legal writing, but that is just another way of saying that good sentences are its foundation. Efficient, persuasive, professional sentences are not only good in and of themselves; they provide a clean workspace for the more difficult task of editing paragraphs, arguments, and briefs. Sometimes drafts, your own or others', that don't seem editable on first read become more tractable once you give their sentences the sorts of makeovers the three preceding chapters have described. If you can apply automatically the "sentencing guidelines" offered herein, you will be well positioned to focus on the more difficult and subtle challenges written advocacy presents, which this book now takes up.

Part Two: The Paragraph

Chapter 5

The Order of Sentences

As the discussion moves from sequencing words in a sentence to sequencing sentences in a paragraph, the terrain becomes more challenging. The difficulty stems in part from the inherently greater complexity of the paragraph, at least as measured by word count. Having more words than a sentence, the paragraph offers more opportunities for some to end up in the wrong place.

But the true reason for the greater difficulty is deeper. The paragraph is an artificial unit of expression. Everyone who speaks articulately speaks in sentences. No one, unless speaking from a prepared text, speaks in paragraphs. English writers did not even begin to employ the paragraph as a formatting device until the Renaissance,[1] and not until the second half of the 18th century did English paragraphs start to follow roughly the same principles that guide their usage today.[2] When, in the Victorian period, scholars of rhetoric started to fashion definitions of the paragraph, the definitions that emerged were fairly broad: *e.g.*, "a collection of sentences with unity of purpose";[3] "a connected series of sentences constituting the development of a single topic."[4]

---

1. *See generally* Edwin Herbert Lewis, The History of the English Paragraph (Univ. of Chicago Press 1894).

2. *Compare* Thomas Hobbes, Leviathan (17th century) *with* James Madison, John Jay & Alexander Hamilton, The Federalist Papers (18th century).

3. Alexander Bain, Manual of English Composition and Rhetoric § 158 (1866).

4. John Franklin Genung, The Practical Elements of Rhetoric 193 (1892).

These broad definitions, which survive to this day,[5] do not fit all forms of prose. Many great fiction writers will sometimes write very long paragraphs spanning ranges of topics not clearly connected to one another. The exceptions have led at least one writing authority to observe that the paragraph's true objective seems to be convenience: to indicate to the reader who needs either to take a break or to resume reading thereafter, where to stop and where to pick up. The paragraph is "something you use for your reader's convenience, rather than as a granitic form laid down by molten logic."[6]

In legal writing, fortunately, the paragraph lends itself, if not to definition, then at least to categorization according to the purpose it serves. If you pay attention to these categories as you draft, you will realize several benefits. Being mindful of the type of paragraph you are writing can help you get the paragraph off to a strong start. It will also help you finish it without getting drawn off onto a tangent. Perhaps most helpfully, and as the next chapter shows, classifying paragraphs will reveal the sequence those paragraphs should follow in an argument. So a small investment in learning to classify paragraphs will pay dividends that will help you meet some of the most important sequencing challenges legal writing presents.

A. Classifying Paragraphs According to Their Purpose

The vast majority of paragraphs in a brief fall into one of three categories—*instructional*, *affirmative*, and *responsive*. To be sure, you will find in a well-written brief paragraphs other these three. A statement of facts will consist entirely of narrative paragraphs, neither referring to nor advocating any legal doctrine or argument. Arguments or preliminary statements may contain paragraphs that summarize arguments to come, without elaboration. Certiorari petitions will often feature paragraphs arguing that circuit splits warrant Supreme Court review, without regard to how the split should be resolved. And amicus briefs exhibit paragraphs of completely different sorts. But to simplify discussion and to help draft the clear majority of the paragraphs the brief-writer needs to write, this three-part scheme will work.

---

5. *E.g.*, "a group of related sentences organized by a single, controlling idea," LEONARD J. ROSEN & LAURENCE BEHRENS, THE ALLYN & BACON HANDBOOK 45 (Longman 5th ed. 2003).

6. SHERIDAN WARNER BAKER, THE COMPLETE STYLIST 61 (Thomas Y. Crowell 1966).

1. Instructional Paragraphs

Instructional paragraphs state and then give relevant additional information about the law governing a dispute (a "legal source"). A legal source may reflect the action of a legislative body (*e.g.*, a statute, a rule, a constitution); an administrative body (*e.g.*, a regulation, a patent claim, an ethics rule); or a court (*e.g.*, case law, court rules). A legal source may also be a contract or another private legal instrument having legal effects, such as a trust or will.

Here is an instructional paragraph:

> *18 U.S.C. § 3161(b) provides in relevant part, "any information or indictment . . . shall be filed within thirty days from the date on which such individual was arrested or served with a summons in connection with such charges." In calculating the 30-day period, the day after which the arrest or service of summons occurred is treated as the first day, and weekends and holidays are counted. See Fed. R. Crim. P. 45(a)(1). The period is extended if the final, thirtieth day falls on a day on which the court in which the charging instrument is to be filed is closed, but not beyond the first day after the court reopens. Fed. R. Crim. P. 45(a)(2)(C).*

Notably, this paragraph does not contain any reference to the parties or to the facts of the case. Nor does it describe or advance a client's position directly. Its tone is calm, confident, and seemingly neutral. It teaches the reader something about the law—and nothing else. It could appear as readily in a treatise as in a brief.

2. Affirmative Paragraphs

Affirmative paragraphs advance a position you want a judge to adopt. They explain one or more reasons why that position is sound. They come in many varieties. Some of the most common

- demonstrate how a legal source, properly interpreted, applies to the facts of a case;
- advance an interpretation of a legal source using linguistic or logical (*e.g.*, syllogistic, proof by contradiction) principles;
- advance an interpretation of a legal source using principles of construction, the source's legislative or drafting history, or other evidence of a drafter's intent;

- argue for a result based on case law;
- articulate prudential ("policy") reasons why a proposed outcome yields a favorable, efficient result; or
- argue, in an appellee's brief, that the lower court ruled correctly on a particular point.

As these examples show, affirmative paragraphs are as diverse as legal arguments themselves. But their defining feature is that if credited, they yield, or at least contribute to, a conclusion or result favorable to your client, without reference to opposing arguments.

Here is an affirmative paragraph that applies the language of a statute to recited facts:

> *Applying 18 U.S.C. § 3161(b), the indictment should be dismissed. The defendant was arrested on May 1, 2022, but the indictment was not filed until June 2. Thus, the period between arrest and filing spanned 32 days, two days beyond the period Section 3161(b) prescribes.*

This paragraph could readily have followed an instructional paragraph like the first example in this chapter. Building upon the law discussed in that prior example, this paragraph applies that law to the facts of the case. Or, if there had been no preceding instructional paragraph, the paragraph could have also described the law:

> *The indictment should be dismissed because it was not timely filed. Under 18 U.S.C. § 3161(b), "any information or indictment . . . shall be filed within thirty days from the date on which such individual was arrested or served with a summons in connection with such charges." The defendant was arrested on May 1, 2022, but the indictment was not filed until June 2. Thus, the period between arrest and filing spanned 32 days, two days beyond the period Section 3161(b) prescribes.*

Even though the second sentence of this paragraph could have appeared in a pure instructional paragraph, the paragraph remains affirmative: it argues for a result. Although instructional paragraphs should never include argument, affirmative paragraphs may contain instructional or narrative material, especially if, as here, the material is short. You may need to briefly restate in an affirmative paragraph facts or legal sources discussed in earlier paragraphs. Or you may need to include facts or information about legal sources not conveniently included in the preceding paragraphs. For example, if you are analogizing your case factually to a precedential case, you should lay out succinctly the analogous facts of your case in the affirmative paragraph drawing the analogy.

Here is an affirmative paragraph that argues for a result based on the holding of a case:

> *Applying 18 U.S.C. § 3161(b), the indictment should be dismissed. The defendant was arrested on May 1, 2022, but the indictment was not filed until June 2. Hence, the period between arrest and filing spanned 32 days, two days beyond the period Section 3161(b) prescribes. Although the court was closed on June 1 and June 2 pursuant to the Covid-19 Lockdown Order, U.S. v. Arnold, 450 F. Supp. 3d 272 (2022), holds that that order did not suspend the operation of the periods prescribed by 18 U.S.C. § 3161(b) because that order did not prohibit or complicate electronic filing.*

Here too, the paragraph contains instructional material—a description of the holding in *Arnold*—that could appear in an instructional paragraph. The paragraph remains affirmative because it argues for a favorable result or conclusion.

Importantly, however, affirmative paragraphs should generally not allude to an adversary's argument. Laying out responsive arguments before you fully lay out your affirmative position can be confusing. What is more, a judge will be more inclined to credit rebuttals of your adversary's position once convinced that your own position is correct. Even when an adversary's argument directly addresses the argument you have laid out in an affirmative paragraph, you should generally take it up later, in a separate paragraph whose sole function is to address the adversary's argument: *i.e.*, a responsive paragraph.

3. Responsive Paragraphs

Responsive paragraphs address arguments an adversary has made or, in some contexts, is expected to make. These paragraphs state that an adversary is wrong and then explain why. Some expose logical fallacies in an adversary's affirmative argument. Others argue that cited legal sources are distinguishable or irrelevant, or that they do not control. Responsive paragraphs are a staple of opposition and reply briefs. They may also appear in opening briefs if a lawyer has decided (after careful consideration) to anticipate an argument an adversary is expected to make. Responsive paragraphs may also appear in *opening* briefs in appeals, where the lower court becomes, in effect, the appellant's adversary, whose reasoning the appellant must persuade the appellate court to reject. They are also common in motions to dismiss claims, as they often restate allegations in a complaint and then explain why they do not state a claim.

Here is an example of a responsive paragraph from an opposition brief:

> *The defendant argues that the indictment should be dismissed because it was not filed within the thirty-day period prescribed by 18 U.S.C. § 3161(b). The defendant is wrong. Although the indictment was filed 32 days after the defendant's arrest, 18 U.S.C. § 3161(h)(1)(E) provides that "delay resulting from any proceeding relating to the . . . removal of any defendant from another district" shall be "excluded in computing the time within which an information or an indictment must be filed." For at least three days within the period that commenced upon the defendant's arrest in the Southern District of Illinois, the defendant was the subject of removal proceedings in that district. If, as is appropriate, those three days are excluded, the filing of the indictment was timely.*

Here is an example of a responsive paragraph from an appellant's opening brief:

> *The District Court declined to dismiss the indictment because it concluded that tolling was authorized for the period attributable to the defendant's removal proceedings. The District Court erred. In B v. C, this court held that the tolling described in 18 U.S.C. § 3161(h) is not authorized when the district from which the defendant is removed, is located within the same state as the district in which the indictment was filed. Applying B v. C, the same result should apply here. As in B v. C, the defendant was arrested in the Southern District of Illinois and removed to the*

> *Northern, where the indictment was filed more than 30 days after his arrest.*

Like affirmative paragraphs, responsive paragraphs often contain instructional material. In opposition and reply briefs, instructional paragraphs at the beginning of arguments often cannot practically include all the legal principles you need to rebut an adversary's disparate arguments; the principles must be stated as needed within each rebuttal. So long as the interpolated instructional material is brief, is on point, and appears in the middle of the paragraph, the paragraph will retain its character as a responsive paragraph. Here is an example of such a responsive paragraph, in which the instructional material appears in bold:

> *The defendant cites U.S. v. Arnold to argue that the Covid-19 Lockdown Order did not relieve the Government of its obligation to file the indictment earlier than June 2. The defendant is wrong.* ***On May 10, 2023, five days after the defendant filed this motion, Arnold was reversed. In reversing, the Court of Appeals held that the Lockdown Order contemplated the tolling of periods even on days on which the court's electronic filing system was operating.*** *Applying the appellate court's holding, the filing of the indictment was timely.*

Here is a template for a responsive paragraph distinguishing a case on its facts. The basis for the distinction requires instructional material, which appears in bold:

> *The defendant cites E v. F to argue that [state proposition]. E is distinguishable.* ***In E, the defendant [describe facts of E].*** *Here, by contrast, the defendant did not [describe facts of instant case].*

When, as here, it is appropriate to describe the facts of a case cited by your adversary, you should keep the description as brief as possible. Rookie writers, understandably eager to impress upon a supervisor the care with which they have read a case, will sometimes describe its facts in lavish detail. As a general matter, aim to describe the facts of a cited case in one or two sentences, and never in more than three. The fewer facts from other cases the judge needs to master, the better.

B. Starting Paragraphs: The "Starter Sentence"

The first challenge in drafting a paragraph is also its most important: you must write a good first sentence. A paragraph that starts out well will propel you forward and simplify the sentence-sequencing challenges that follow. Conversely, paragraphs that start with a poor first sentence are much harder to edit; in truth, they often need to be rewritten from scratch. They are like a horse that stumbles out of the gate: they cannot finish well.

To draft a good first sentence for a paragraph—the "starter sentence"—you must appreciate that it has a specific function to perform and that that function varies depending on the type of paragraph you are writing. You can and should use different words to perform that function. But if a starter sentence, however worded, does not fully serve the function specific to the paragraph it leads off, the remainder of the paragraph will likely prove hard to write.

This section identifies the function of the starter sentence for each type of paragraph and offers examples of such sentences. It then presents an example illustrating how the different types of starter sentences might appear in a full argument.

1. Starter Sentences for Instructional Paragraphs

The starter sentence for an instructional paragraph has one goal: to identify the legal provision or principle on which the lawyer will rely:

> *Article 3.4(c) of the Contract states, ". . . ."*
>
> *In 1987, the SEC promulgated Rule 17-c, which provides, ". . . ."*
>
> *In Charles v. Robert, the Supreme Court held that ". . . ."*
>
> *Under the doctrine of federal preemption, no state law may ". . . ."*

Starter sentences for instructional paragraphs conform to this model for a simple reason: before learning what a legal source means or how it applies, the judge must know what it is and what it says.

In drafting such starter sentences, you should, when possible, quote rather than paraphrase the legal provision, principle, or holding on which you rely. Although a quote may not always be the clearest or shortest statement, you need, especially early in an argument, to build credibility with the judge, and that will generally counsel quoting, rather than paraphrasing, the legal source. Judges have been misled by slanted restatements of law so often that they are instinctively suspicious of paraphrase. They will not always appreciate the help you are trying to give them in recasting what may be dense legal language as clear prose. It is fine, especially when up against a word limit, to excerpt the quoted provision, using ellipses or brackets to indicate deletions or substitutions. But avoid paraphrase as much as possible.

Sometimes paraphrase cannot be avoided. Case holdings may not be stated concisely, or they may be stated in a way that makes them hard to understand outside the context of the opinion in which they arise. Some general legal doctrines may not have authoritative statements that you can readily quote. In these situations, a neutral, unimpeachably accurate paraphrase is necessary. But when discussing statutes, regulations, contracts, trusts, wills, or patent claims, you should teach the decision-maker about them using the original texts. You can defer explaining their complexities to the sentences that follow.

2. Starter Sentences for Affirmative Paragraphs

The starter sentence for an affirmative paragraph comes in many varieties. But it must perform at least one function: to indicate the position you will be advocating in that paragraph. The simplest merely state that position:

> *The complaint should be dismissed.*
>
> *Applying D v. E, the complaint should be dismissed.*
>
> *Under the doctrine of claim preclusion, the complaint should be dismissed.*
>
> *Defendant's contributory negligence defense should be stricken.*
>
> *The legislative history of the statute supports Plaintiff's reading.*
>
> *This Court's case law supports the outcome Plaintiff seeks.*

The starter sentence for an affirmative paragraph may then go on to offer at least one reason for that position, often using the most important word English offers the litigator: *because*.

> *The complaint should be dismissed because it fails to state a claim upon which relief may be granted.*
>
> *As in A v. B, the complaint should be dismissed because none of its allegations describes with particularity the "who, what, when, and where," Albert v. Bernard, at 234, of the alleged misstatement.*
>
> *Consistently with the foregoing principles, the complaint should be dismissed because it does not state that any investor invested in reliance on the April 3 Misstatement.*
>
> *The complaint should be dismissed because the facts on which it is based are identical to those upon which the complaint in the prior action was based.*
>
> *Even if the Court rejects the foregoing arguments, it should still grant the motion because the motion's denial would lead to an absurd result.*

Whether to incorporate a because-clause within the starter sentence will often turn on whether, to understand a reason, the judge must appreciate some legal principle or background fact not covered in a preceding instructional paragraph. If so, laying out the reason in a because-clause may bog down the starter sentence with too much detail:

> *The complaint should be dismissed because B v. D holds that . . . . In B v. D, ... So too here, ... Accordingly, and by analogy to B v. D, the complaint should be dismissed.*

Better here to dispense with a because-clause:

> *The complaint should be dismissed under the holding of B v. D. In B v. D, ... So too here, ... Accordingly, and by analogy to B v. D, the complaint should be dismissed.*

But even if, as in this example, you choose not to articulate the reason for the paragraph's conclusion with a because-clause, that sentence should at least state that conclusion.

3. Starter Sentences for Responsive Paragraphs

Starter sentences for responsive paragraphs have two goals: to inform the judge of the position the lawyer is rebutting and to signal that rebuttal will immediately ensue. To do that, the starter sentence, in its most basic form, is, in fact, two sentences. The first will be called the *target sentence*; the second, the *denial sentence*. The combination will be referred to as the *target-denial setup*.

✦ The Target Sentence

The first, target sentence focuses the reader on the argument you are targeting for rebuttal: the clay pigeon toward which the responsive argument is aimed. Here is the basic form of the target sentence for a responsive paragraph:

Adversary argues X.

As with the starter sentence for instructional paragraphs, it is often preferable in the target sentence to quote your adversary's position rather than to paraphrase it; not because the adversary has written it well (he rarely has) or fairly (never!), but, again, because quoting the argument helps you build credibility with the judge. The judge will presume that any paraphrase of an adversary's argument will be tendentious and hence misleading. By quoting the argument in relevant part, you steer clear of that presumption and bolster your reputation as a lawyer the judge can trust:

Adversary argues ". . . ."

Adversary cites C *v.* D *for the proposition that* ". . . ."

Quoting the adversary's argument also serves an additional purpose in opposition or reply briefs. It helps the judge recall more precisely and more quickly to which arguments, among the thicket of arguments she has just read in the adversary's brief, you are now turning.

That said, quoting an adversary's argument is often not feasible or advisable. An adversary's argument is sometimes so badly written that quoting it does not help the judge understand your rebuttal. By paraphrasing the argument, you may gain favor with the judge subconsciously, by helping her to understand better your ensuing rebuttal. Or even if an adversary's argument is clearly stated, it may appear in a context in which it does not lend itself to quotation, or it may be so general and simple that quoting it would be awkward ('*Defendant argues that "this action is time-barred."*'). Here too, paraphrase is preferable. Or you may be up against a word limit that makes it necessary to save room for your own argument by shortening the target sentence in a responsive paragraph. But in all such instances, any paraphrase should be as neutral and precise as possible. The paraphrase of the argument should never carry any slant. A *fortiori*, it should not be accompanied by bombastic adverbs like *absurdly*, *frivolously*, *astoundingly*, etc. The sole goal of the target sentence is to state the adversary's argument in a way that lends itself to immediate understanding. The rest of the paragraph will show why it is absurd.

✦ The Denial Sentence

The second, denial sentence announces that the lawyer disagrees with the position articulated, without stating in detail why. The basic form of the denial sentence for a responsive paragraph appears in bold:

Adversary argues X. ***Adversary is wrong.***

You might consider the denial sentence superfluous in the context of advocacy, where it goes without saying that the lawyer disagrees with an adversary's positions. It is generally not. True, the denial sentence in its simplest form does not provide the judge with meaningful information, but it nonetheless plays a role. It is serving as a prompt for the judge to change mental gear and to prepare to evaluate your own argument why your adversary is wrong. For the judge who needs to read quickly, that gear-change prompt helps. Without a denial sentence, the judge may need to read a few words of the ensuing sentence or even further into the paragraph to appreciate that the lawyer has finished setting up his target and has now moved on to shooting it down:

> *Reagan argues that the Boise City Code treats exceptions for buildings exceeding Boise's height limitations differently from how it treats other exceptions to the Code's permit provisions. Other than citing provisions of the Code that give height exceptions different names, Reagan does not cite any provision of the Code that sets forth a different standard for evaluating permits for such buildings.*

The judge could be forgiven for not appreciating until well into the second sentence that that sentence is rejecting the paraphrase of Reagan's argument in the first. With a brief denial sentence wedged between the two sentences, that momentary confusion never arises:

> *Reagan argues that the Boise City Code treats exceptions for buildings exceeding Boise's height limitations differently from how it treats other exceptions to the Code's permit provisions.* ***That argument, however, lacks support in the text of the Code.*** *Other than citing provisions of the Code that give height exceptions different names, Reagan does not cite any provision of the Code that sets forth a different standard for evaluating permits for such buildings.*

The target-denial setup comes in many varieties, but none strays from the basic model. For a paragraph addressing an argument that is not based on case law, the following are common variants:

> *Adversary argues X.* ***Her argument is misguided.***

> *Adversary argues X.* ***The Court should reject this argument.***

> *Adversary argues X.* ***Adversary, however, misstates the facts upon which his argument is based.***

> *Adversary argues X.* ***The argument proves too much.***

> *Adversary argues X.* ***But the argument does not withstand scrutiny because nothing in the statute supports that conclusion.***

Similarly, for a paragraph addressing a case an adversary has cited, here are common variants of the target-denial setup:

> *Adversary cites C v. D for the proposition that . . . .* ***Adversary wrongly relies on this case.***

> *Adversary cites C v. D for the proposition that . . . .* ***Adversary's reliance on this case is misplaced.***

> *Adversary cites C v. D to argue that . . . .* ***C v. D is not on point.***

> *Adversary cites C v. D to argue that . . . .* ***His argument should be rejected because C v. D does not control.***

> *Adversary cites C v. D to argue that . . . .* ***The facts of C v. D distinguish it from the facts here.***

Innumerable other variants of the denial sentence exist, so long as, again (see Chapter 3, The Persuasive Sentence, at pp. 58–59), you avoid the common fault of bombast:

> *Adversary argues X.* ~~*His argument is fatally flawed.*~~
>
> *Adversary argues X.* ~~*Her argument is absurd.*~~
>
> *Adversary argues X.* ~~*The argument is frivolous.*~~

Especially with simpler target-denial setups, you can often compress the target and denial sentences into one:

> *Adversary wrongly argues X.*
>
> *In arguing X, adversary misstates the record.*
>
> *Adversary's reliance on C v. D to argue X is misplaced.*

This compression technique can be effective, especially in meeting a word limit. But you should use it judiciously, as it can sometimes pack too much information into a sentence that ought to be getting the paragraph off to a smooth start. Better to draft the starter sentence for a responsive paragraph as separate target and denial sentences. Then, if warranted, edit them down to a single sentence later.

Because the argument sections of many opposition and most reply briefs primarily rebut an adversary's disparate and often sprawling arguments, the two-sentence target-denial setup recommended here can lead to fairly tedious prose. There are ways to vary the tedium of a series of paragraphs that all begin '*Plaintiff/Defendant argues X. X is wrong,*' some of which the preceding exemplary sentences illustrate. Once you have completed a draft of an opposition or reply brief, you can revise it to modify or supplement the starter sentences to break up the tedium. For example, it may sometimes be helpful, before a target-denial setup, to restate the overall result for which you are advocating:

> *No severance should be granted. Defendant Y argues that a severance is warranted because co-trial with Defendant*

> *Z will deprive him of his right to offer certain evidence. Defendant Y is wrong.*

Or you may preface the target-denial setup with a lead-in that indicates the general category into which the rebuttal will fall:

> *The cases Plaintiff cites do not advance his argument. Plaintiff argues that D v. E. . . .*

But in departing from the target-denial setup, be mindful that more bracing prose may less well serve the judge, who has a mental list of arguments that she wants to be able to cross off one by one as they are addressed. The target-denial setup helps the judge to perform this cross-off exercise. It also gives a judge, as she reads an opposition or reply brief, the confidence that she is dealing with a lawyer who has carefully considered every argument his adversary has made and who has thoughtful things to say to rebut each one. This is yet another instance in which goals that take precedence in other types of writing yield to a unique goal of brief-writing: to help a judge get a job done.

A final aside on the topic of denial sentences. For all the reasons that lawyers should use them liberally, judges should probably eschew them in their starkest form. The power and status of a judge are such that explicit statements that a litigant's position is wrong or that a lower court judge reasoned incorrectly can come across as bullying or gratuitously hostile. For example, Chief Justice Roberts did well to begin this responsive paragraph criticizing an argument advanced by a respondent and four dissenting colleagues as he did here, with only a target sentence:

> *Maine and the dissents invoke Locke v. Davey, 540 U.S. 712 (2004), in support of the argument that the State may preclude parents from designating a religious school to receive tuition assistance payments. In that case, Washington had established a scholarship fund . . . .*

He was probably right not to put a denial sentence (*e.g.*, '*Maine and the dissents are wrong to rely on Locke for this argument.*') after the target sentence, even though a denial sentence would have been well placed if he had been writing a brief attacking the respondent's position.

4. Starter Sentences–Examples

To show how a moderately complex argument benefits from starter sentences performing the functions identified earlier, here is a sample, simplified argument advancing the petitioner's position in the 2023 Supreme Court case *Bittner v. United States*. *Bittner* concerned whether, under the Bank Secrecy Act, a person who unintentionally fails to report to the IRS the existence of multiple accounts held at a non-U.S. bank faces a maximum civil penalty whose amount turns on the number of unreported accounts held at that single bank or, instead, solely on the value of the person's aggregate holdings at the bank. The majority opinion, together with its dissenting opinion by Justice Barrett (joined by Justices Thomas, Sotomayor, and Kagan), is reported at 598 U.S. 85 (2023). The following exemplary argument does not come from any brief filed in the case or the opinions; it has been drafted solely to illustrate how to draft instructional, affirmative, and responsive paragraphs and the starter sentences (in bold) associated with each.

> **Instructional Paragraph: *Under the Bank Secrecy Act (the "BSA"), Congress directed the Secretary of the Treasury to "require a resident or citizen of the United States . . . to file reports . . . when the [person] makes a transaction or maintains a relation for any person with a foreign financial agency." 31 U.S.C. § 5314(a).*** *The regulations the Secretary promulgated pursuant to the BSA require such persons to file a Foreign Bank Account Report ("FBAR") when the balance in one or more of their non-U.S. ("foreign") bank accounts exceeds $10,000. 31 C.F.R. §§ 1010.350(a), 1010.306(c). For a non-willful violation of the FBAR-filing requirement, the Act prescribes a civil penalty of not more than $10,000. 31 U.S.C. § 5321(a)(5)(A)–(B).*
>
> **Affirmative Paragraph: *The judgment below should be reversed because the BSA contemplates that the maximum penalty for non-willful conduct will be calculated without regard to whether the funds held at a single foreign bank are held in a single account or in multiple accounts.*** *Section 5314(a) of the BSA defines the source of the obligation to file a "report" as a "transaction" or "relation" with a foreign bank. Once such a "transaction"*

or "relation" exists, a violation occurs only if the required, compliant "report" is not filed. Id. And that violation is single, not several, even if the report fails to comply for several reasons. Thus, a report that fails to report $50,000 spread over five separate accounts or the same amount held in a single account gives rise in either instance to a single violation of Section 5314(a). To that single violation, so understood, the civil penalty cap of $10,000 per non-willful violation applies.

Affirmative Paragraph: *Other provisions of the BSA confirm that a violation of Section 5314(a) results from a failure to file a complete, compliant annual report rather than every error or omission the incomplete, non-compliant annual report may contain.* *Under Section 5321(a)(5)(C) & (D), the amount of the penalty for "willful violations" is "in the case of a violation involving a failure to report the existence of an account . . . , [50 percent of] the balance in the account at the time of the violation." This "account balance" cap on the penalty for willfully concealing "the existence of an account" reflects Congress's appreciation that even when the violation involves completely and deliberately concealing an account, the penalty for that, the most serious misconduct Section 5314(a) reaches, should not turn on the number of unreported accounts but on the amount of the unreported funds in each. That amount bears far more significantly on culpability than the number of accounts holding the funds.*

Affirmative Paragraph: *The regulations the Secretary promulgated to implement Section 5314(a) also confirm that penalties for failing to file an FBAR should not turn on the mere number of unreported accounts.* *31 C.F.R. § 1010.350(a) requires the annual filing of a single form, TD F 90-22.1, and that requirement turns on the aggregate, not individual, account balance. What is more, the regulations do not even require the filer to list each account if the number of accounts exceeds 24. 31 C.F.R. § 1010.350(g). If the IRS cares to know only the aggregate amount of funds held at each foreign bank, and not also the number of accounts among which the holder* *allocated the funds, it is not clear why a court fashioning a penalty for non-willful misconduct should take that latter, essentially arbitrary figure into account.*

Affirmative Paragraph: *In contrast to the reading advanced here, the alternative reading the Fifth Circuit endorsed yields results that, if not absurd, would at least call into question the rationality of the BSA's penalty provisions.* *Under the Fifth Circuit's reading, a person who inadvertently fails to file any FBAR for the single account she holds at a single foreign bank faces a lower maximum penalty, no matter how much the account holds, than a person who diligently files an FBAR but innocently omits to include a few of the several accounts she holds there. That "partial filer" faces a higher penalty than the non-filer even if the amounts held in her few unreported accounts are small compared to the amounts held in the accounts she did report. Similarly, the holder of, say, five unreported accounts, each holding $10,000, faces a higher maximum penalty ($50,000) than the holder of a single unreported account holding $500,000. The latter faces a maximum penalty of only $10,000. Those results and others like them are avoided only by the reading advanced here, under which the maximum penalty for an innocent failure to file a complete, correct FBAR cannot exceed $10,000.*

Affirmative Paragraph: *Most lower courts have adopted the reading of Section 5321 advanced here.* *In United States v. Boyd, 991 F.3d 1077 (9th Cir. 2021), a divided panel of the Ninth Circuit held that Section 5321 authorizes only one penalty per unfiled or incomplete FBAR, no matter how many accounts are held at the foreign bank to which the FBAR relates. The Ninth Circuit based its holding primarily upon Congress's notable failure, when it amended the BSA to include penalties for non-willful violations, to make the cap on those penalties resemble the existing cap on penalties for willful violations. Id. at 1083. The cap on the latter, willful penalties treats each failure to report an account as a separate violation, 31 U.S.C. § 5321(a)(5)(D)(ii), permitting a reasonable inference that* *for non-willful violations, a different treatment was intended. United States v. Kaufman, No. 18-787, 2021 WL 83478 (D. Conn. Jan. 11, 2021), and United States v. Giraldi, No. 20-2830, 2021 WL 1016215 (D.N.J. Mar. 16, 2021), reached the same conclusion, as did the district court in this case. See United States v. Bittner, 469 F. Supp. 3d 709 (E.D. Tex. 2020).*

Responsive Paragraph: ***The government argues that to affirm, "this Court need look no further than the text of Section 5321(a)(5) itself." Govt. Br. at 22. Yet that text does not answer the question presented.*** *To be sure, Section 5321(a)(5) authorizes penalties for non-willful "violations" of Section 5314. But neither that section nor Section 5314 offers a definition of the "violation" to which penalties may attach. And even if the BSA could be read to imply a definition under which each failure to report a distinct account constituted a distinct "violation" of the BSA, it would not follow that the penalty cap prescribed by Section 5321(a)(5)(B)(i) would make the number of unreported accounts an integer by which maximum penalties might be multiplied without limit.*

Responsive Paragraph: ***The government also argues that limiting the cap on non-willful violations to $10,000 per non-compliant FBAR "would significantly curtail the Secretary [of the Treasury]'s ability to make penalties more proportional to the harms represented by the underlying violations." Govt. Br. at 40. That argument is not persuasive because it assumes that Congress intended to vest the IRS with such vast penalty-calibrating power.*** *For all the textual, contextual, and prudential reasons identified earlier, Congress intended to limit strictly the penalties the IRS could impose upon innocent violators. Giving the IRS additional discretion to ratchet up penalties by $10,000 multiples of however many accounts the innocent violator held would thwart that congressional intent.*

* * *

Many well-written arguments will have paragraphs whose starter sentences do not clearly resemble any of the examples offered herein. The appearance of such deviant paragraphs does not necessarily mean that the argument is badly written. Nor does it mean that the guidance offered here is flawed or incomplete. You will encounter situations in which you may sensibly depart from the guidance. For example, you may preface the starter sentence with a short sentence or subordinate clause designed to enhance the flow of the argument or to show the judge that the argument is taking a different direction. But as a new writer or as an experienced editor facing a deadline, you will find that knowing the basic starter sentence you can count on to get any paragraph in an argument off to a serviceable start is a valuable skill. You may even find, when faced with a draft with poorly structured paragraphs, that merely recasting each paragraph with the standard starter sentence will tame the draft and make it more editable. Once the draft is edited, you can then modify some of the draft's prosaic starter sentences or precede them with phrases or sentences that enhance the flow of the overall argument or give it more flair.

5. False Exceptions

Two common formatting practices can sometimes make it seem as if the lawyer is not writing good starter sentences when in fact she is.

✦ Argument Headers as Starter Sentences

Because standard argument headers generally state a desired result or conclusion and because they initiate arguments, they tend also to be good starter sentences. For that reason, lawyers will sometimes start the ensuing paragraph as if the argument header had been its first, starter sentence. In the following affirmative paragraphs, the headings serve also as the starter sentences:

> **1. *The Insurers Have Not Shown That Western's Claim Falls Within the Exception for Faulty Workmanship.***
>
> *Under Georgia law, the Insurers have the burden to show that Western's claim falls within the faulty workmanship exclusion. The Insurers have failed to meet their burden. . . .*

Or:

> ***a. Trial Counsel's Performance Prejudiced Reeves.***
>
> *To prove prejudice, Reeves "must show that there is a reasonable probability that but for counsel's unprofessional errors, the result of the proceeding would have been different." Strickland, 466 U.S. at 694. Under this standard, Reeves's ineffective assistance claim succeeds. . . .*

This practice is commendable, as it prevents what might otherwise be needless repetition of a well-crafted starter sentence for an affirmative paragraph. The practice tends to work best for third- or fourth-level headings, rather than higher. For higher-level argument headings, some repetition or, better, rephrasing of the heading itself can often be an effective way to get an argument off the ground:

> ***C. The Complaint Fails to Plausibly Allege That MG Engaged in an Act of International Terrorism.***
>
> *The Third Claim for Relief fails for the independent reason that Plaintiffs do not allege that MG committed, as required under the Anti-Terrorism Act, an "act of international terrorism."*

But even higher-level headings can serve as the starter sentence for the first paragraph under the heading. This can be especially helpful if a word limit is pressing.

✦ False Paragraph Breaks

Lawyers, compelled by court rules to double-space and to use large font sizes, will find that paragraphs requiring more than a few sentences often create the visual impression of a cramped page. The practice unique to legal writing of putting citations, often lengthy and laden with dense parentheticals, into the body of the text rather than in footnotes can exacerbate the impression. So to counter it, lawyers will often break up a long paragraph to create more bite-size paragraphs. There is nothing wrong with this practice. Again, the paragraph is itself an artificial formatting device, and breaking up blocks of text to help propel the judge to the end may be a favor he appreciates. In following the guidance this chapter offers, you should write paragraphs containing as many sentences as you need to make your argument. Then, later, feel free to break up a paragraph at convenient incision points if, after careful editing, it still looks too bulky.

C. The Rest of the Paragraph

So you've started a paragraph strongly. Now what? You have to finish it. In drafting the ensuing sentences of a paragraph, you have essentially two goals, and they are the same no matter what type of paragraph you are writing. The paragraph should convey the impression that its sentences are logically connected to one another; the sentences should create a sense of flow. In addition, the sentences, as a group, should hang together; they should give the reader the sense of a discussion that is on topic and does not wander off onto tangents. These two goals are distinct. A paragraph may have good flow but nonetheless qualify as incoherent:

> *In 2024, Congress enacted the Large Warehouse Artificial Intelligence Act. That act, when drafted, regulated the development of artificial intelligence devices useful in managing inventory in large warehouses. Such devices help inventory managers detect inventory shrinkage, a common problem in multilevel warehouses. Multilevel warehouses make up 34% of all warehouses in the United States, a percentage greater than the percentage of such warehouses in other developed countries, including in the EU. In the EU, large warehouses make up only 25% of all warehouses, and no law regulates artificial intelligence devices of any kind.*

By the same token, a focused paragraph may nonetheless seem choppy and disjointed:

> *This case concerns the drug arenonate. Arenonate treats fungal infections of the skin. Dermatologists prescribe arenonate. Arenonate is prescribed as a tablet or a capsule. Patients take the tablet twice daily and the capsule twice daily. The tablet should be taken with food. The capsule can be taken with or without food. The tablet contains 50 mg of arenonate. The capsule contains 75 mg of arenonate. The patented, capsule form is the subject of U.S. Patent No. 9,887,455.*

Several devices and principles help the legal writer enhance flow and coherence. In the preceding chapters, this book has already discussed two: logical traffic signals and lookback. This chapter now turns to a technique alluded to earlier but on which discussion was deferred: varying sentence length.

1. Varying Sentence Length

Chapter 2 (The Efficient Sentence) criticized the common, unqualified advice to keep sentences short. It instead recommended that the length of a sentence should be commensurate with the complexity of its ideas. When structuring paragraphs, that recommendation remains sound, but you will find in every credible guide to style, non-legal and legal, an additional pointer: vary the lengths of the sentences within a paragraph. Good paragraphs, whether in legal or non-legal prose, non-fiction or fiction, generally consist of a mix of sentences that are relatively long and relatively short. Indeed, the legal scholar and rhetorician Ward Farnsworth has offered data suggesting that readers may consider some judges better stylists than others partly because of the variance in the lengths of their sentences.[7] Certainly Holmes's skill in alternating long and short sentences was part of what made him a transcendent legal stylist:

> *In deciding this question we must realize that however ancient may be the traditions of maritime law, however diverse the sources from which it has been drawn, it derives its whole and only power in this country from its having been accepted and adopted by the United States. There is no mystic overlaw to which even the United States must bow. When a case is said to be governed by foreign law or by general maritime law that is only a short way of saying that for this purpose the sovereign power takes up a rule suggested from without and makes it part of its own rules. Also we must realize that the authority that makes the law is itself superior to it, and that if it consents to apply to itself the rules that it applies to others, the consent is free and may be withheld. The sovereign does not create justice in an ethical sense, to be sure, and there may be cases in which it would not dare to deny that justice for fear of war or revolution. Sovereignty is a question of power, and no human power is unlimited. But from the necessary point of view of the sovereign and its organs whatever is enforced by it as law is enforced as the expression of its will.*
>
> *The Western Maid, 257 U.S. 419 (1922)*

---

7. Ward Farnsworth, Classical English Style 64–73 (Godine 2020).

Long—Short—Long—Long—Long—Short—Long.

A concern in offering the uncontroversial advice to vary the lengths of sentences is that you will deliberately strive for long–short sentence patterns in your paragraphs in the way that Greek and Latin poets strove for long–short vowel patterns in their verse. That is a bad practice because paragraphs that rigidly alternate long and short sentences tend not to read well. The better approach is to recast the advice negatively. Instead of *Vary the lengths of sentences*, recast the prescription as a proscription: *Avoid having too many long or short sentences in a row*. Paragraphs may bog down or seem choppy if the writer has placed more than a few long or short sentences in series. If you see either in an otherwise well-constructed paragraph, consider breaking up a sentence or two, or combining some.

2. Reducing Sprawl

Another concern is that by consciously trying to vary the lengths of sentences, you will lengthen some sentences by introducing sprawl, the impression of a sentence that meanders. Sprawl comes not just from unnecessary words; those can be eliminated easily. Sprawl that is harder to tame comes from sentences composed of multiple clauses:

> *Thus, in a situation like this, in which Armstrong does not seek review of any cease-and-desist order and instead seeks to enjoin ongoing constitutional violations, the various APA provisions read together affirmatively authorize declaratory and injunctive relief from a "court of competent jurisdiction," which precisely describes a district court exercising its jurisdiction under Section 1331.*

This sentence can be improved by eliminating unnecessary words:

> *Thus, as here, where Armstrong does not seek review of a cease-and-desist order but instead seeks to enjoin constitutional violations, the APA authorizes declaratory and injunctive relief from a "court of competent jurisdiction," which describes a district court exercising jurisdiction under Section 1331.*

But even after the shearing, the sprawl remains.

To address sprawl, consider the guidance offered in the referenced non-legal writing texts.[8] They offer suggestions on which this book cannot improve for using the various devices English offers—subordinate clauses, appositives, participial phrases, summative modifiers, etc.—for increasing the length and complexity of a sentence without generating sprawl. The best writers will seem to effortlessly craft sentences with these syntactical structures, to add relevant information without superfluity or throat-clearing.

Lincoln was a master at this:

> *Either the opponents of slavery will arrest the further spread of it, and place it where the public mind shall rest in the belief that it is in the course of ultimate extinction; or its advocates will push it forward, till it shall become alike lawful in all the States, old as well as new, North as well as South.*
>
> SPEECH AT SPRINGFIELD (*1858*)
>
> *It is rather for us to be here dedicated to the great task remaining before us: that from these honored dead we take increased devotion to that cause for which they gave the last full measure of devotion; that we here highly resolve that these dead shall not have died in vain; that this nation, under God, shall have a new birth of freedom; and that government of the people, by the people, for the people, shall not perish from the earth.*
>
> GETTYSBURG ADDRESS (*1863*)
>
> *With malice toward none, with charity for all, with firmness in the right as God gives us to see the right, let us strive on to finish the work we are in, to bind up the nation's wounds, to care for him who shall have borne the battle and for his widow and his orphan, to do all which may achieve and cherish a just and lasting peace among ourselves and with all nations.*
>
> SECOND INAUGURAL ADDRESS (*1865*)

---

8. JOSEPH M. WILLIAMS, STYLE: TEN LESSONS IN CLARITY AND GRACE 107–47 (Univ. of Chicago Press 3d ed. 1989) ("Controlling 'Sprawl,' Managing Long Sentences"); LEONARD J. ROSEN & LAURENCE BEHRENS, THE ALLYN & BACON HANDBOOK 376–78 (Longman 5th ed. 2003) ("Strategies for Varying Sentence Length"); SHERIDAN WARNER BAKER, THE COMPLETE STYLIST 97–105 (Thomas Y. Crowell 1966) ("Compound and Complex Sentences").

In the modern era and in the field of law, Richard Posner is a standout:

> *While a single precedent is a fragile thing—apt to be distinguished away, ignored, or rejected by a coequal or superior court or even by the same court on a later occasion—an accumulation of precedents dealing with the same question will often create a rule of law having virtually the force of an explicit statutory rule.*
>
> THE ECONOMIC ANALYSIS OF LAW *(1986)*

> *And—to return to my last suggestion concerning the springs of his greatness—he owed those principles not to legal texts or other traditional sources of law but to the possession of a philosophical mind that saw the Darwinian struggle, for example, instantiated in the labor movement, the social-welfare movement, and even communist agitation; that insisted on subjecting legal doctrine to the pragmatic test of meaning; that built judicial restraint and freedom of speech on the surprisingly robust foundations of skepticism, relativism, and pragmatism; that distinguished with unprecedented clarity between legal positivism and natural law.*
>
> THE ESSENTIAL HOLMES *(1992)*

> *Many of the cases that arise in our dauntingly complex, uncertainty-riven legal system—featuring an antique constitution, an overlay of federal on state law, weak political parties, cumbersome and undisciplined legislatures, and executive-legislative tugs of war (so unlike the situation in parliamentary regimes)—cannot be decided by the straightforward application of a preexisting rule.*
>
> HOW JUDGES THINK *(2008)*

The best additional advice for making paragraphs flow well and coherently—and hinted at in the last few paragraphs—is to immerse yourself in the prose of the best persuasive writers, both non-legal and legal. The goal is not to consciously imitate their style when writing. Especially if the stylist is not modern, even successful imitations will come off as odd. The goal is instead, like a child learning a new language, to acquire language skills passively and in contexts in which the brain will subconsciously learn to apply them in other contexts in which they should be practiced. If this seems like a cop-out in a writing text, perhaps. But consider that the greatest stylists probably acquired their skill in the same way: by voraciously reading prose of high quality. Those whom we call gifted writers may simply be writers who accepted at an early age the gifts that well-written prose affords those who take the time to read it.

* * *

To properly sequence the sentences in a paragraph of an argument, you must above all understand the purpose the paragraph will serve in the argument. The vast majority of paragraphs in an argument serve one of three purposes: instructional, affirmative, or responsive. For each of these types of paragraphs, a standard type of starter sentence helps to launch the paragraph. Once launched, the paragraph will proceed and finish well if you can maintain its focus and show how neighboring sentences relate to each other. Varying sentence length within the paragraph will also help make the paragraph give off a more natural impression that most readers will associate with good prose style.

Part Three: The Argument

Chapter 6

The Order of Paragraphs

Getting the order of paragraphs in an argument right is the most important challenge the lawyer must meet in a draft intended for editorial review. An argument that is well organized but lacks strong sentences or individual paragraphs can be edited efficiently with the guidance of the earlier chapters. A poorly organized argument, even one whose paragraphs and sentences are efficient and elegant, cannot. The process of rearranging paragraphs and making the edits necessary to hide the stitches is generally so inefficient and fraught that many editors will scrap the draft and rewrite it from scratch. This process creates significant workplace tensions. It makes junior lawyers tasked with drafting feel inadequate. It makes senior lawyers tasked with editing their work want to retire. In private law firms, the process can increase the client's bill in ways that even the most mercenary lawyer does not intend.

Unlike the challenges taken up in the preceding chapters, the challenge of sequencing paragraphs in an argument is not verbal or stylistic; it is analytic. To meet it you must understand the contentions underpinning the argument and how they logically relate to one another. Many lawyers, including many very good lawyers, derive these relations intuitively. But the process lends itself to analysis and thus to instruction. One overarching principle controls the process, and a few other, subordinate principles simplify those aspects that remain.

With help from the principles explained in this chapter, you will be able to prepare a detailed outline that will guide drafting just as blueprints guide builders. This is important, for just as no competent builder would ever start to build a house without a blueprint, so too you should never—ever—start to draft even the simplest brief without a carefully thought-out outline. And if you are asking another lawyer to draft a brief for you to edit, you should insist first on an outline, and you should force yourself to review it thoughtfully before letting any drafting begin.

To facilitate this chapter's discussion, two terms will be defined and distinguished. The terminology is not standard, but the distinction it permits, once grasped, will be familiar to most litigators:

1. **Contention:** As used in this chapter, a "contention" means:

   The demonstration of either

   (i) a single legal principle or

   (ii) a single fact

   that supports a desired conclusion or outcome.

The first type of demonstration will be referred to as a **legal contention**; the second, a **factual contention.**

Examples of legal contentions would be

- a demonstration that a statute punishes certain conduct with a fine;
- a showing that the drafting history of a statute supports a contested interpretation of the statute; and
- an assertion that the meaning of a term in one contractual provision supports assigning it the identical meaning in a different, contested provision.

Examples of factual contentions would be

- a showing through the testimony of an eyewitness that a person engaged in certain conduct;
- proof by reference to a transcript that a party made a particular statement; and
- a demonstration based on the opinions in an expert report that a substance causes a disease.

A contention, legal or factual, may require only one sentence:

> *Under Penal Code § 213.4, a person who drives a vehicle through a red light commits an infraction punishable by a fine not to exceed $1,000.*

or:

> *According to A's testimony, B drove through the light at the intersection while the light was red. (Tr. 312)*

But more commonly, a contention, especially one that is contested, requires a paragraph. Sometimes a contention may even require more than one paragraph, but when it does, that can be a telltale sign that the single contention has more than one within it. This is not just a matter of sterile intellectual interest; it has practical consequence. Distinguishing between single and multiple contentions is a critical aspect of outlining, as outlining consists essentially of identifying an argument (as next defined) and then filling in lower levels of the outline with the individual legal and factual contentions that establish it.

2. **Argument:** In contrast with a contention, an "argument" means:

> *The demonstration, based on at least one legal contention and at least one factual contention, that a fact or a set of facts has a practical legal consequence that is favorable to your client's position.*

Thus, the defining feature of an argument is that it combines at least one legal and at least one factual contention to derive a conclusion you want a judge to draw. Or, as litigators say, an argument applies law to facts to reach a result. An argument in this special sense is what most litigators mean when they refer to the multi-paragraph passages that fall under the high, primary- (I., II., etc.) and secondary-level entries (A., B., etc.) of a brief's table of contents. Lawyers will also refer to the subsidiary propositions that this chapter will call "contentions" as arguments too, without any sacrifice of precision. But in this chapter, "argument" will refer only to the larger unit of advocacy just defined.

Note that the definition of an argument calls for at least one of each type of contention. An argument can and often does derive conclusions based on more than one legal and/or more than one factual contention. In some types of arguments (*e.g.*, motions to dismiss pleadings, submissions advocating for or against proposed jury instructions, appellate arguments), the legal contentions will dominate, either because the facts are undisputed or because they must be assumed or taken as established. In other types of arguments (*e.g.*, summary judgment arguments, arguments attacking the sufficiency of trial evidence, pre-charging submissions to a prosecutorial agency), factual contentions may be more numerous and dominate. But if an argument lacks at least one legal contention and at least one factual contention, it is something else.

Here, derived from two of the earlier exemplary contentions, is an argument in its simplest form:

> *Under Penal Code § 213.4, a person who drives a vehicle through a red light commits an infraction punishable by a fine not to exceed $1,000. According to A's testimony, B drove through the light at the intersection while the light was red. For this reason, B must pay a fine.*

This simple, three-sentence paragraph satisfies the definition of an argument. It has at least one legal contention: the first sentence; at least one factual contention: the second sentence; and in the third sentence, it states a practical legal consequence: a fine. The practical legal consequence could also be something purely procedural, like the dismissal of a claim or, conversely, allowing a claim to stand. Or it could be something intangible or abstract, such as a finding that satisfies or disproves an element of a claim or offense. But the consequence, whatever its nature, must have some practical legal effect by itself, alone and without combination with other facts or legal principles.

It follows from the definition of an argument that a fully stated argument always requires at least three sentences, as in the example of the last paragraph. In this respect, an argument is like a syllogism, to which it is similar. But arguments as simple as this three-sentence example are rare. Nearly all arguments encountered in practice require several paragraphs, each serving important functions. These several paragraphs will, among other things,

- lay out the legal framework governing the dispute, even when the governing principles are not disputed;

- lay out the factual background necessary to follow the argument, to the extent the background has not already been laid out in a preceding background statement;
- offer a reason or, more often, reasons why the law should be interpreted in a manner that favors your client's position;
- apply the law, favorably interpreted, to a set of facts, by showing either how undisputed or assumed facts yield a desired result, or how disputed facts either are irrelevant or should be resolved in your client's favor;
- offer alternative arguments, which compel a desired outcome even if others do not; and
- in many submissions, explain why the contentions or arguments your adversary has made are wrong or irrelevant.

This very long sentence, formatted with bullet points to aid understanding, gives a sense of the challenges you will face in organizing all the contentions that comprise arguments litigated in the real, messy world.

Fortunately, one overarching principle to tame these challenges exists:

Teach first–Argue later.

Teach first–Argue later (hereafter, TFAL) means that in laying out any argument, you should first identify and explain (*teach*) the facts and legal principles the judge needs to know to rule for your client. Teach those fully, confidently, and, above all, calmly and non-argumentatively before you draft any sentence that advocates a disputed reading or result. After that, argue fully, with zeal and power. Lay out your affirmative arguments. Lay out your alternative arguments. And in opposition, reply, and, occasionally, opening submissions, lay out your responsive arguments rebutting the arguments your adversary has made or that you anticipate he will make. But do all this *later*.

If you peruse a brief selected at random, you will find that lawyers at every level and in every specialty disregard TFAL all the time. That commonly happens in statements of facts, where the lawyer prematurely includes argument or presents the facts in an argumentative way. But lawyers also regularly disregard TFAL in the argument sections of briefs, where they launch into argument before teaching the judge the law or certain facts she needs to know. Sometimes that is because the lawyer is facing tight word limits; or because he trusts that the judge knows the law or remembers the facts recited in some prior submission. But more often, it is because the lawyer has not outlined his argument carefully in advance to make sure that teaching occurs before arguing.

The disregard of TFAL and not putting the most important idea at the end of a sentence (see Chapter 3, The Persuasive Sentence, at p. 38) are by far the most pervasive errors in legal writing. But of these two very common errors, launching into argument mode prematurely is the more serious. Failing to conclude a sentence with its most important idea will deprive a sentence of some of the persuasive force it could exert, but if the sentence is otherwise well constructed, it will at least be comprehensible. Failing to teach the judge fully before launching into argument reliably generates arguments that are hard to follow at best and incoherent at worst. No one can follow an argument unless he first understands the facts and law that inform its evaluation.

A. 'Teach'

In an opening or initial opposition brief, the standard structure of the brief will help you follow TFAL. The standard opening or opposition brief includes introductory sections that lay out the historical or procedural facts or scientific or technical issues the judge must understand to follow the arguments. Some also contain background sections describing some of the law that the remainder of the brief will discuss. Because these sections invariably come before the argument sections of the brief, their placement forces you to *Teach first*.

But no matter how extended the background sections, the argument section of the brief will still call for a fair amount of teaching. The last chapter offered advice for how to draft the instructional paragraphs that embody most of that teaching. The point to emphasize here is that instructional paragraphs should always come first. To see why, compare two versions of the following extract from a brief filed by the insured in a coverage dispute. In derogation of *Teach first*, the first version places an arguing paragraph *before* a teaching paragraph:

I. The Corrosion Exclusion Does Not Preclude Coverage for Damage from the Chlorine Gas Explosion.

The Insurers argue that the Policy contains a "broad exclusion for corrosion" that bars coverage. The Insurers are wrong.

A. The Exclusion Does Not Apply Because the Damage Was Caused by an Explosion.

[Arguing Paragraph] *The policy does not exclude coverage for the damages the Insured incurred because of the Explosion. As is standard within the insurance industry, the Corrosion Exclusion includes corrosion as one of several non-fortuitous, gradual forms of "wear-and-tear." Under Georgia's doctrine of noscitur a sociis, corrosion damage should be understood to refer only to damage that is similarly gradual. For this reason, the damage from the April 4 chlorine explosion qualifies for coverage under the Policy even assuming for the sake of argument that the underlying cause of the instantaneous explosion was gradual corrosion of the chlorine gas's tank.*

[Teaching Paragraph] *This conclusion is clear from review of the language of the Corrosion Exclusion itself. Section 5.4 of the Policy provides in relevant part:*

> *"This policy does not insure against loss, damage or expense resulting from . . . loss or damage from wear and tear, rust, corrosion, erosion, depletion or gradual deterioration, but not excluding resultant physical loss or damage from a covered peril." Policy Section 5.4.*

"Corrosion" is not defined in the policy, nor is "resultant physical loss."

By contrast, in the following version and in accord with TFAL, the instructional, teaching paragraph comes first and the affirmative, arguing paragraph later:

I. The Corrosion Exclusion Does Not Preclude Coverage for Damage from the Chlorine Gas Explosion.

The Insurers argue that the Policy contains a "broad exclusion for corrosion" that bars coverage. The Insurers are wrong.

A. *The Corrosion Exclusion Does Not Apply Because the Damage Was Caused by an Explosion.*

[Teaching Paragraph] *Section 5.4 of the Policy (the "Corrosion Exclusion") provides in relevant part:*

> *"This policy does not insure against loss, damage or expense resulting from . . . loss or damage from wear and tear, rust, corrosion, erosion, depletion or gradual deterioration, but not excluding resultant physical loss or damage from a covered peril."*

"Corrosion" is not defined in the policy, nor is "resultant physical loss."

[Arguing Paragraph] *As the text of Section 5.4 shows, the Corrosion Exclusion does not exclude coverage for the damages the Insured incurred because of the Explosion. Like similar exclusions in similar contracts, the Corrosion Exclusion includes corrosion as one of several non-fortuitous, gradual forms of "wear-and-tear." Under Georgia's doctrine of noscitur a sociis, "corrosion" damage should be understood to refer only to damage that is similarly gradual. For this reason, the damage from the April 4 chlorine explosion qualifies for coverage under the Policy even assuming for the sake of argument that the underlying cause of the instantaneous explosion was gradual corrosion of the chlorine gas's tank.*

The sequence of paragraphs in the second version is superior because it does not call upon the judge to evaluate the force of the insured's interpretive argument until he knows the law—Section 5.4—that will apply. By contrast, the first version asks the judge, in essence, to trust that the policy language will support the argument stated in the heading. At that juncture, the judge has no reason to place in the lawyer such trust. The lawyer must earn that trust by, first, quoting the policy language accurately and, second, helpfully letting the judge know that she should not spend time searching for a policy definition of '*corrosion*' or '*resultant physical loss*.' Knowing those things, the judge will be more inclined to credit the canonical ('*noscitur a sociis*') argument for construing '*damage from . . . corrosion*' when that argument first appears. In this way, TFAL not only better serves the judge—it gives her a chance to learn necessary material just before she needs it most—but also better serves you, the lawyer. It gives you a chance to build credibility with the judge just before you need it most: when you start arguing.

In trying to *Teach first*, try to teach judges only what they do not already know, for judges often complain that briefs belabor principles and rules with which they are very familiar. *E.g.*, the standard for summary judgment under Fed. R. Civ. Proc. 56; the standard for relevance under Fed. R. Evid. 402. When the judge is experienced and the issue you are briefing is a staple of her docket, you can generally manage the risk of boring or patronizing her. The risk assessment gets harder if the judge is new to the bench. There is also the distinct challenge of writing for intermediate appellate courts, which typically assign judges to an appeal only after briefs are submitted. And even when you know the judges who will be reading your brief, you will often know nothing about the clerks who will be helping them.

In all these recurring situations, you have to somehow avoid crossing the line that separates helpful teaching from superfluous lecturing. To stay on the right side, consider whether the judge's or the court's opinions frequently lay out the same basic point of law you need to teach. If so, omit the point. Or, if omitting it would be awkward, state it without elaboration and pare down the accompanying string cites. Above all, resist the temptation to recycle boilerplate that you found in other briefs. Their discussions of basic legal points may be well written and well researched, but having been written for other cases and generally for other judges or courts, they are rarely a perfect fit for the brief you are writing.

Roadmap Paragraphs: In tension with *Teach first* is the practice of placing summary paragraphs at the outset of arguments. Many lawyers do this with endorsement from legal writing authorities. Here is an example of two such summary, "roadmap" paragraphs (in bold) from a brief about the application of the Free Exercise Clause to a state law regulating private school tuition assistance:

> *I. Maine's Exclusion Violates the Free Exercise Clause*
>
> ***Maine's exclusion violates the Free Exercise Clause. It is neither religiously neutral nor generally applicable and, for that reason, must be subjected to strict scrutiny. Under strict scrutiny, Maine's exclusion does not survive.***

> ***Contrary to the Circuit Court's decision, there is no basis for failing to apply strict scrutiny on the theory that the exclusion discriminates based upon religious use rather than religious status. Neither the Free Exercise Clause's text nor this Court's decision in Locke v. Davey warrants such a use/status distinction. To the extent Locke intended to imply a constitutionally meaningful distinction, it was wrongly decided and should be overruled.***
>
> A. *Maine's Exclusion Is Subject to Strict Scrutiny Because It Is Neither Neutral nor Generally Applicable.*
>
> *"A law burdening religious practice that is not neutral or not of general application must undergo the most rigorous of scrutiny"—namely, strict scrutiny—and "will survive such scrutiny only in rare cases." Church of the Lukumi Babalu Aye, Inc. v. City of Hialeah, 508 U.S. 520, 546 (1993). The Court reiterated these criteria only last term in Fulton v. City of Philadelphia, 141 S. Ct. 1868, 1877 (2021), and made clear that they apply where, as here, the burden on religious exercise comes from the withholding of an otherwise available public benefit. Id. . . .*

Placing the two paragraphs in bold at the outset of the argument offends TFAL because the paragraphs argue for conclusions. In general, and despite their support from many legal writing authorities, you should avoid these sorts of extended roadmap or "umbrella" paragraphs at the outset of an argument. Although a judge wants to know where an argument is headed, argument headings, if well constructed like those in the preceding example, will adequately serve that interest. The detail contained in the opening summary paragraphs is superfluous to the detail of the paragraphs in the ensuing argument. The summary paragraphs may also be redundant of summaries set forth in an introduction to a brief or a formal summary of argument.

Redundancy, however, is not the only problem. Roadmap paragraphs like those in the last example are poorly placed for a judge who has not yet learned from the brief the full meaning of concepts like '*religiously neutral*' and '*generally applicable*,' the full holding of *Locke v. Davey*, or the contour of the use–status distinction *Locke* purportedly draws. The principle of TFAL proceeds primarily from the conviction that judges are more likely to credit arguments if they first understand their underpinnings. Executive summary paragraphs stand at odds with that conviction.

Granted, a short, framing paragraph nestled between a major heading and a minor heading is a fairly minor inroad upon TFAL:

> II. *Maine's Exclusion Violates the Free Exercise Clause.*
>
> ***Maine's exclusion violates the Free Exercise Clause. It is neither religiously neutral nor generally applicable and, for that reason, must be subjected to strict scrutiny. Under strict scrutiny, Maine's exclusion does not survive.***
>
> A. *Maine's Exclusion Is Subject to Strict Scrutiny Because It Is Neither Neutral nor Generally Applicable.*
>
> . . .

The inroad is tolerable and avoids the minor inelegance of two headings not separated by text. Similarly, you might choose to preface an argument with a very short roadmap paragraph or, better, sentence when you have a major heading stating a result (*e.g.*, '*I. This Action Should Be Dismissed.*'), followed by minor headings (A., B., C.) setting forth the different reasons for the result. In that situation, and space permitting, you may want to frame the argument with a simple sentence along the lines of:

> I. *The Action Should Be Dismissed.*
>
> ***This action should be dismissed for three reasons: the defendant lacked a duty to plaintiff; the plaintiff did not suffer a compensable injury; and the action is time-barred.***
>
> A. *The Defendant Lacked a Duty to Plaintiff.*
>
> . . .

Positioned between the first major (I.) and minor (A.) headings, this prefatory sentence operates more to elaborate the argument headings. As such, it does not seriously offend TFAL. But prefatory paragraphs that go beyond mere restatements of the argument headings are best left for a standalone summary of argument. Some appellate courts require such summaries, and some require them to appear after the brief's statement of the case or statement of facts. That is a good place for them to appear because, in accord with TFAL, that placement teaches the dispute's facts before summarizing what the brief will argue.

B. 'Argue'

Once you have finished teaching, some subordinate principles organize the arguing that should now take center stage. Although these principles are not as strong as TFAL—you will encounter situations in which you will want to depart from them—they are nonetheless helpful to understand as you outline the second phase of every argument.

1. Place Legal Contentions Before Factual.

The first subordinate principle of argument organization is to place legal contentions before factual, without regard to whether the argument's legal or factual contentions are more significant, numerous, or sharply contested. The trial lawyer's adage that *when the law is against you, argue the facts* (and vice versa) has force, but only in the context of oral advocacy. When reading written advocacy, a judge expects (1) law to be applied to (2) facts to reach (3) a conclusion. In writing arguments, you should accommodate this expectation.

To see why, consider again the simple exemplary argument from the beginning of this chapter:

> *Under Penal Code § 213.4, a person who drives a vehicle through a red light commits an infraction punishable by a fine not to exceed $1,000. According to A's testimony, B drove through the light at the intersection while the light was red. For this reason, B must pay a fine.*

You could revise it to:

> *According to A's testimony, B drove a vehicle through the light at the intersection while the light was red. Under Penal Code § 213.4, a person who drives a vehicle through a red light commits an infraction punishable by a fine not to exceed $1,000. For this reason, B must pay a fine.*

so that the factual contention appears before the legal. The argument is still coherent. But the revision makes the argument somewhat more difficult to follow because the judge temporarily wonders why she is learning that, according to A, B drove through a red light. The fault is not serious here, in this very simple argument about a law everyone knows. But with even moderately more complex arguments where the governing law may be unfamiliar, the fault can meaningfully impair understanding.

The standard way to bridge between legal contentions and factual contentions is with a starter sentence along the lines of:

> *Applying these principles, the Court should . . . .*

Or with a sentence beginning with a transitional phrase to similar effect:

> *In accord with this doctrine, . . .*
>
> *Under the statute, so interpreted, . . .*
>
> *Applying the holding of Y v. Z, . . .*

Here, for example, is a simple two-paragraph argument in which the first paragraph lays out the legal contentions, and the second lays out the factual. In this example, the factual contentions about a hurricane are not disputed.

> **[Legal Contentions]** *Under Article 4.7 (Force Majeure), "any delay in or failure of performance . . . will be excused to the extent caused by any occurrence beyond the reasonable control of such party including, . . . hurricanes. . . ." In Texas, hurricanes qualify as force majeure events, even when the tropical disturbance is classified only as a "tropical storm" for part of the day on which performance was required. Warnaco v. Royal Insurance Co., 347 S.W.3d 347 (Tex. 2011).*
>
> **[Factual Contentions]** *Applying Article 4.7, Defendant was excused from the obligation to deliver the goods before September 12, 2022. Under Fed. R. Evid. 201, the Court may take judicial notice of the records of the National Weather Service, showing that on that date, the Houston regional area experienced a Category 1 hurricane, Hurricane Chloe. In no submission, including its complaint, has Plaintiff denied that Hurricane Chloe occurred or that it affected the delivery Defendant failed to make by September 12.*

> **[Practical Legal Consequence]** *Accordingly, Defendant's performance should be excused because Hurricane Chloe constituted a force majeure event.*

The discussion of the factual contentions will become longer if the plaintiff contests them or their effect:

> **[Legal Contentions]** *Under Article 4.7 (Force Majeure), "any delay in or failure of performance . . . will be excused to the extent caused by any occurrence beyond the reasonable control of such party including, . . . hurricanes. . . ." In Texas, hurricanes qualify as force majeure events, even when the tropical disturbance is classified only as a "tropical storm" for part of the day on which performance was required. Warnaco v. Royal Insurance Co., 347 S.W.3d 347 (Tex. 2011).*
>
> **[Factual Contentions]** *Applying Article 4.7, Defendant was excused from the obligation to deliver the goods before September 12, 2022. There is no dispute that Hurricane Chloe made landfall in Houston on September 12. Plaintiff alleges this in its complaint and Defendant admitted it.*
>
> **[Factual Contentions]** *Instead, Plaintiff contends that at the time Defendant's ship was supposed to enter Houston Harbor, the hurricane—then classified as a tropical storm—was still far offshore. Defendant's position does not withstand scrutiny. To be sure, Defendant's meteorology expert opined that Tropical Storm (later Hurricane) Chloe was interfering with cargo shipments only after 10 a.m. on the morning of September 12, 2022. But the expert acknowledged under cross-examination that in formulating his opinion, he had not considered the ship's records showing that on September 11, the ship's captain, responding to a Coast Guard warning, detoured his ship to avoid sailing into the course of (then) Tropical Storm Chloe. And although Defendant's expert on navigation acknowledged at his deposition that the ship could have reached the Port of Houston safely if it had simply increased its speed towards Houston as soon as it received the September 11 Coast Guard warning, Defendant's expert nonetheless opined that failing to heed the warning would have deviated from the standard of care for merchant marine*

> *vessel captains. What is more, he observed that it might have also compromised the insurance covering the voyage.*
>
> **[Practical Legal Consequence]** *Accordingly, Defendant's performance should be excused because Hurricane Chloe constituted a force majeure event.*

In both examples, the first in which the facts are uncontested, the second in which they are contested, the legal contentions appear before the factual.

2. Group Related Contentions Together.

The second subordinate principle is that in advancing or rebutting contentions, groups of related contentions should appear together. This sounds sensible, even uncontroversial. In fact, it is. But it calls for a concept of relatedness that, surprisingly, has not developed within the U.S. legal profession. Just what, in the context of brief-writing, does it mean to say that contentions *relate* to one another?

To answer that question, this book now suggests a system for classifying legal and factual contentions. For the vast majority of arguments, this system will give you what you need to structure an argument. For more complicated arguments (or if you have a jurisprudential bent), this book offers a supplementary, more detailed taxonomy of legal and factual contentions (see pp. 179–184).

Here is the simpler system:

✦ Related Legal Contentions

Two or more legal contentions relate to one another if they all fall into one of three classes: *interpretive*, *precedential*, or *prudential* (also referred to as *policy* or *pragmatic*).

Interpretive contentions argue that a legal source (*e.g.*, statutes, cases, contracts, wills; see Chapter 5, The Order of Sentences, at p. 73) means something because of what its words say. The simplest example is a contention that the source says something expressly or "plainly," or at least with the aid of a general dictionary. Another example of an interpretive contention argues that the source should be interpreted in a certain way because of the purpose it seeks to achieve; interpreting it differently would thwart that purpose. When interpretive contentions are not disputed, they are typically set forth in instructional paragraphs.

More complex interpretive contentions argue that a legal source means something in light of its surrounding words or of how other related legal sources (*e.g.*, regulations, contracts) are written. Interpretive contentions can also argue for interpretations advanced by experts (*e.g.*, proposed constructions of patent claims) or by the judge(s) in the same action (*i.e.*, through a prior ruling, such as an appellate ruling when the case goes back to the lower court on remand) to mean what you are now contending it means.

Precedential contentions argue that a legal source means something because an opinion in a *different* case has assigned it that meaning. They argue that an earlier case has created a rule of decision to apply here. If the case arose on facts similar to those of the instant case, the similarity may be invoked to argue that the case applies by analogy.

Prudential contentions argue that the court should interpret a legal source to avoid reaching a result that would be unfair, inefficient, or absurd. The threatened unfairness, inefficiency, or absurdity could arise in litigation of the instant action, in litigation of future actions, or in society as a whole. Prudential contentions draw force not from the content of the legal source they interpret but from the favorable consequences that will flow from interpreting the source in a particular way.

Most well-developed arguments will draw upon a variety of legal contentions falling into each of these three broad classes. Keeping related contentions together means that in advancing the contentions affirmatively or responsively, you should group together all contentions falling into the same class. Here, drawing again upon the arguments presented in *United States v. Bittner* (see Chapter 5, The Order of Sentences, at p. 86), is a sample argument grouping the legal contentions together in the manner suggested:

> **Instructional Paragraph (Undisputed Interpretive Contentions):** *Under the Bank Secrecy Act (the "BSA"), Congress directed the Secretary of the Treasury to "require a resident or citizen of the United States . . . to file reports . . . when the [person] makes a transaction or maintains a relation for any person with a foreign financial agency."*

31 U.S.C. § 5314(a). The regulations the Secretary promulgated pursuant to the BSA require such persons to file a Foreign Bank Account Report ("FBAR") when the balance in one or more of their non-U.S. ("foreign") bank accounts exceeds $10,000. 31 C.F.R. §§ 1010.350(a), 1010.306(c). For a non-willful violation of the FBAR-filing requirement, the act prescribes a civil penalty of not more than $10,000. 31 U.S.C. § 5321(a)(5)(A)–(B).

Affirmative Paragraph (Interpretive Contentions): *The judgment below should be reversed because the BSA contemplates that the maximum penalty for non-willful conduct will be calculated without regard to whether the funds held at a single foreign bank are held in a single account or in multiple accounts. Section 5314(a) of the BSA defines the source of the obligation to file a "report" as a "transaction" or "relation" with a foreign bank. Once such a "transaction" or "relation" exists, a violation occurs only if the required, compliant report is not filed. Id. And that violation is single, not several, even if the report fails to comply for several reasons. Thus, a report that fails to report $50,000 spread over five separate accounts or the same amount held in a single account gives rise in either instance to a single violation of Section 5314(a). To that single violation, so understood, the civil penalty cap of $10,000 per non-willful violation applies.*

Affirmative Paragraph (Interpretive Contentions): *Other provisions of the BSA confirm that a violation of Section 5314(a) results from a failure to file a complete, compliant annual report rather than every error or omission the incomplete, non-compliant annual report may contain. Under Section 5321(a)(5)(C) & (D), the amount of the penalty for "willful violations" is "in the case of a violation involving a failure to report the existence of an account . . . , [50 percent of] the balance in the account at the time of the violation." This "account balance" cap on the penalty for willfully concealing "the existence of an account" reflects Congress's appreciation that even when the violation consists of completely and deliberately concealing an account held at a foreign bank, the penalty for that, the most serious* *misconduct Section 5314(a) reaches, should not turn on the number of unreported accounts but on the amount of the unreported funds in each. That amount bears far more significantly on culpability than the number of accounts holding the funds.*

Affirmative Paragraph (Interpretive Contentions): *The regulations the Secretary promulgated to implement Section 5314(a) also confirm that penalties for failing to file an FBAR should not turn on the mere number of unreported accounts. 31 C.F.R. § 1010.350(a) requires the annual filing of a single form, TD F 90-22.1, and that requirement turns on the aggregate, not individual, account balance. What is more, the regulations do not even require the filer to list each account if the number of accounts exceeds 24. 31 C.F.R. § 1010.350(g). If the IRS cares to know only the aggregate amount of funds held at each foreign bank, and not also the number of accounts among which the holder allocated the funds, it is not clear why a court fashioning a penalty for non-willful misconduct should take that latter, essentially arbitrary figure into account.*

Affirmative Paragraph (Prudential Contentions): *In contrast to the reading advanced here, the alternative reading the Fifth Circuit endorsed yields results that, if not absurd, would at least call into question the rationality of the BSA's penalty provisions. Under the Fifth Circuit's reading, a person who inadvertently fails to file any FBAR for the single account she holds at a single foreign bank faces a lower maximum penalty, no matter how much the account holds, than a person who diligently files an FBAR but innocently omits to include a few of the several accounts she holds there. That "partial filer" faces a higher penalty than the non-filer even if the amounts held in her few unreported accounts are small compared to the amounts held in the accounts she did report. Similarly, the holder of, say, five unreported accounts, each holding $10,000, faces a higher maximum penalty ($50,000) than the holder of a single unreported account holding $500,000. The latter faces a maximum penalty of only $10,000. Those results and others like* *them are avoided only by the reading advanced here, under which the maximum penalty for a non-willful failure to file a complete, correct FBAR cannot exceed $10,000.*

Affirmative Paragraph (Precedential Contentions): *Most lower courts have adopted the reading of Section 5321 advanced here. In United States v. Boyd, 991 F.3d 1077 (9th Cir. 2021), a divided panel of the Ninth Circuit held that Section 5321 authorizes only one penalty per unfiled or incomplete FBAR, no matter how many accounts are held at the foreign bank to which the FBAR relates. It based its holding primarily upon Congress's notable failure, when it amended the BSA to include penalties for non-willful violations, to make the cap on those penalties resemble the existing cap on penalties for willful violations. Id. at 1083. The cap on the latter, willful penalties treats each failure to report an account as a separate violation, 31 U.S.C. § 5321(a)(5)(D)(ii), permitting a reasonable inference that for non-willful violations, a different treatment was intended. United States v. Kaufman, No. 18-787, 2021 WL 83478 (D. Conn. Jan. 11, 2021), and United States v. Giraldi, No. 20-2830, 2021 WL 1016215 (D.N.J. Mar. 16, 2021), reached the same conclusion, which is also the conclusion the district court reached in this case. See United States v. Bittner, 469 F. Supp. 3d 709 (E.D. Tex. 2020).*

Responsive Paragraph (Interpretive Contentions): *The government argues that to affirm, "this Court need look no further than the text of Section 5321(a)(5) itself." Govt. Br. at 22. Yet that text does not answer the question presented. To be sure, Section 5321(a)(5) authorizes penalties for non-willful "violations" of Section 5314. But neither that section nor Section 5314 offers a definition of the "violation" to which penalties may attach. And even if the BSA could be read to imply a definition under which each failure to report a distinct account constituted a distinct "violation" of the BSA, it would not follow that the penalty cap prescribed by Section 5321(a)(5)(B)(i) would make the number of unreported accounts an integer by which maximum penalties might be multiplied without limit.*

> **Responsive Paragraph (Prudential Contentions):** *The government also argues that limiting the cap on non-willful violations to $10,000 per non-compliant FBAR "would significantly curtail the Secretary [of the Treasury]'s ability to make penalties more proportional to the harms represented by the underlying violations." Govt. Br. at 40. That argument is not persuasive because it assumes that Congress intended to vest the IRS with such vast penalty-calibrating power. For all the textual, contextual, and prudential reasons identified earlier, Congress intended that to limit strictly the penalties the IRS could impose upon innocent violators. Giving the IRS additional discretion to ratchet up penalties by $10,000 multiples of however many accounts the innocent violator held would thwart that congressional intent.*

To formally complete the argument, you would add the requisite factual contention and practical legal consequence: "*Because Bittner's 2012 failure to report the five accounts he held at a foreign bank was not willful, the maximum penalty to which he may be subject is $10,000.*"

If, after you have grouped related legal contentions together, you find that your argument requires more than one type of group (as in the preceding argument), you must determine a sensible order in which to present the groups.

As a general matter, the strongest legal contentions tend to be interpretive, so they typically appear first. Precedential contentions tend to be more forceful after the judge understands on his own, and without guidance from case law, why the reading you have advanced makes sense linguistically and logically. In most disputes about the meaning of a disputed term in a statute, contract, regulation, etc., case law will only corroborate what is fundamentally an argument why principles of interpretation compel the reading you advance.

Also as a general matter, prudential contentions should follow interpretive and precedential. No matter how forceful prudential contentions are—and they are often extremely forceful—U.S. judges tend to be wary of relying primarily on arguments rooted in notions of why a proffered reading contributes to the smoother, more efficient, and fairer functioning of the legal system or the world as a whole. Yes, legal realists and pragmatists argue that in deciding cases, judges in fact defer more to these prudential, outcome-driven considerations than to considerations of "plain meaning" or *stare decisis*. (And they may well be right. This book takes no view on this important jurisprudential issue.) But to say this is not to say that you should, in organizing your argument, depart from the conventional view that judges should resolve disputes solely in accord with the meaning of legal texts or the dictates of case law. *E.g.*, the "balls and strikes" metaphor of Chief Justice John Roberts; *Fiat justitia, ruat caelum* (Let justice be done though heaven falls). If nothing else, judges like to think of themselves as impartial arbiters, so leading with textual and precedential contentions caters to that preference.

But the suggestions offered in the last two paragraphs are just generalizations. You will often want to depart from them, and that may well be the right thing to do. If a case's holding resolves how to interpret a legal source, then that may be a good reason to lead with a precedential contention based on that case. Your interpretive contentions then merely confirm how well the controlling case's reading dovetails with the reading the text of the legal source compels. Similarly, if a prudential contention (*e.g.*, '*Statutes should be construed to avoid unconstitutionality*.') is so persuasive and well accepted that common law has elevated it to a canon of construction, that may be a good reason to lead with it.

✦ Related Factual Contentions

Factual contentions appear in written advocacy less commonly than legal. That is because facts, when they need resolution, generally get resolved through oral testimonial proceedings. But there are still many contexts in which lawyers argue about facts in writing. Perhaps the most common examples are summary judgment briefs, where the nub of the dispute is always whether certain facts are genuinely disputed, or post-trial briefs after a bench trial, in which the parties advocate for specific factual findings. A less obvious example is an expert report. Expert reports are ostensibly written by experts, not lawyers, but expert reports can often read like briefs in support of various factual contentions because that, in a sense, is what they are.

Two or more factual contentions relate to one another if they all fall into one of three classes: *indisputable*, *uncontradicted*, or *contradicted/ambiguous*.

Indisputable factual contentions are factual assertions that your adversary is not permitted to contradict even if she can. Examples are facts that the court must accept as true in a certain context. The most common examples are allegations addressed in a motion to dismiss, in which the court must generally treat all plausibly alleged facts as true:

> *Plaintiff alleges in the complaint that on April 2, 2011, Defendant struck him with a bat.*

Other examples are facts established earlier in the instant action (*e.g.*, through an appeal) or preclusively in earlier, resolved actions involving the same parties (*i.e.*, issue preclusion):

> *In accord with the Eighth Circuit's decision, Plaintiff has established through the prior proceedings that on April 2, 2011, Defendant struck him with a bat.*

Though fairly rare, factual contentions established through unrebuttable presumptions also qualify as indisputable.

Uncontradicted factual contentions are factual assertions that your adversary is permitted to contradict but cannot because no evidence contradicts them. Whether the fact is in fact uncontradicted is often hotly contested, but if *you* contend that it is uncontradicted, that makes the contention uncontradicted for the purposes of at least your opening brief:

> *Witness X testified that Defendant struck Plaintiff with a bat on April 2, 2011, and Defendant's counsel did not cross-examine X on that point.*
>
> *Expert Witness Y opined that the car's skid marks indicate that the Defendant applied the brakes when the car was traveling at a speed of 85 m.p.h., and Defendant's expert Z has offered no opinion on that issue.*
>
> *Plaintiff alleged in his complaint that the assault occurred on April 2, 2011, and Defendant admits the date in his answer.*

Contradicted/ambiguous factual contentions are those factual assertions whose accuracy the parties dispute: *e.g.*, whether, in a trial for rape, the victim consented; whether, in a securities fraud trial, a public statement was false and, if so, whether the falsehood was material; whether, in a patent infringement case, a machine practices a patented feature of the claimed invention. Contradicted/ambiguous factual contentions are the staple of trials and arbitrations. The vast majority of closing arguments present lawyers sparring over which factual contentions the jury should credit and which, in a bench trial, the judge should find as facts.

It is not challenging to organize separate groups of disputable factual contentions if they concern only one fact. In that simple situation, the right sequence puts the uncontradicted first and the contradicted/ambiguous second. Here is a simple example from a hypothetical opposition to a motion for a judgment of acquittal after a vehicular homicide trial. In this example, the single fact asserted is: *the Defendant was driving at more than 80 m.p.h.*

> **Uncontradicted Contentions:** *Defendant committed aggravated vehicular homicide, 29 Ohio Rev. Code 2903.06, because when he drove through the intersection, he was driving "recklessly": at a speed in excess of 80 m.p.h. The District Attorney's expert witness on accident reconstruction testified that the skid marks the car left past the site at which the victim lay unconscious indicated that Defendant had applied his brakes while traveling at a speed of at least 80 m.p.h., possibly higher. Tr. 1023. The expert also opined that the significant injuries the unbuckled back seat passenger suffered when Defendant applied the brakes were consistent with a vehicle traveling at such a high speed and inconsistent with travel at a lower. Id. at 1029. Notably, Defendant did not call any expert witness to offer a different opinion.*
>
> **Contradicted Contention:** *The District Attorney's expert also opined, on cross-examination, that the failure of the impact of the dog in the front seat to shatter the windshield as the car decelerated was consistent with his conclusion. Tr. 1108. Although the defense attempted to show through cross-examination that standard windshield glass cannot withstand the impact of a 50 lb. dog propelled forward at the speed posited by the prosecution, the prosecution's expert noted that many cars manufactured after 2018 contain reinforced glass, capable of resisting such impacts. Id. at 1113. The defense offered no evidence that Defendant's car lacked such reinforced glass. As a result, the jury was entitled to credit the expert's otherwise unchallenged opinion.*

> **Ambiguous Contention:** *The District Attorney also offered eyewitness testimony from Ann Harris, who was standing at the northeast corner of the intersection when the accident occurred. She testified that Defendant's vehicle was traveling at a "very high speed." Tr. 290. Although she admitted on cross-examination that she could not be "certain" that the speed exceeded 80 m.p.h., she testified on re-direct that she thought the car was traveling at a speed more "like what I see when I look at a highway." Id. at 310. The jury was entitled to credit that testimony also.*

When, however, an argument relies on multiple factual contentions, organization becomes more challenging. Unfortunately, this challenge is common. Crimes have several elements, each of which turns on a different factual contention. Patent claims have several limitations, infringement of each of which must be shown. In a fraud case, the defendant will often be alleged to have made several false statements, each of which individually can give rise to liability. Etc.

Often a sensible order will suggest itself after you appreciate that some facts are members of a more general set of facts. A con artist may have committed credit card fraud hundreds of times, but if she used only five cards held by five different victims, the identity of the card or of the victim offers a grouping principle. If, on the other hand, you have to argue about sets of facts that don't fit under neat headings, then standard ordering principles like chronological order (earlier to later) or complexity (simple to complex; general to specific) can help. Because of the infinite variety, novelty, and complexity of the facts that get litigated in the real world, it is hard to offer general tips for organizing arguments that require advocacy about several facts.

3. Placement of Factually Similar Cases

When organizing arguments, a recurring issue is where to discuss factually similar cases. In some briefs, there will be none to discuss, but in many there will be some or many. In these briefs, you must consider why you are citing or discussing the factually similar case. That will help determine where to discuss it.

If a factually similar case states a seminal legal contention, then the holding of the case should be treated simply as a precedential legal contention and, as such, grouped with related legal contentions. To return to the earlier example:

> *Under Article 4.7 (Force Majeure), "any delay in or failure of performance . . . will be excused to the extent caused by any occurrence beyond the reasonable control of such party including, . . . hurricanes. . . ."* ***In Texas, hurricanes qualify as force majeure events, even when the tropical disturbance is classified only as a "tropical storm" for part of the day on which performance was required. Warnaco v. Royal Insurance Co., 347 S.W.3d 347 (Tex. 2011).***

If, in contrast, you can establish all the legal contentions you need without discussing all the factually similar cases, then you might appropriately defer their discussion until you have laid out all the factual contentions to which you need to apply the law. In that common situation, you are using the cases more to confirm the soundness of the result for which you are advocating than to teach the judge the law. By concluding your argument with a line of factually similar cases reaching the same result you seek, you give the judge confidence that the conclusion she has just drawn from reading your argument is the same conclusion other judges, faced with similar cases, have drawn too. This is the approach the next example follows. While *Warnaco* is cited at the beginning to establish the core legal contention, discussion of similar cases is tacked on at the end, after that contention has been applied to the facts:

> *Under Article 4.7 (Force Majeure), "any delay in or failure of performance . . . will be excused to the extent caused by any occurrence beyond the reasonable control of such party including, . . . hurricanes. . . ." In Texas, hurricanes qualify as force majeure events, even when the tropical disturbance is classified only as a "tropical storm" for part of the day on which performance was required. Warnaco v. Royal Insurance Co., 347 S.W.3d 347 (Tex. 2011).*
>
> *Applying Article 4.7, Defendant was excused from the obligation to deliver the goods before September 12, 2022. Under Fed. R. Evid. 201, the Court may take judicial notice of the records of the National Weather Service, showing that on that date, the Houston regional area experienced a*

> *Category 1 hurricane, Hurricane Chloe. In no submission, including its complaint, has Plaintiff denied that Hurricane Chloe occurred or that it affected the delivery Defendant failed to make by September 12.*
>
> ***Several courts in Texas have reached similar conclusions on similar facts. In Arthurson v. National Marine Ins. Co., 371 S.W.3d 47 (Tex. App. 2014) (Category 1 hurricane), the court excused the shipper's performance. To similar effect, Field Tracking Co. v. Albion Surety Co., 372 S.W.3d 234 (Tex. App. 2014) (Category 2 hurricane, but downgraded to Tropical Storm upon landfall), declined to award damages for late delivery. And in Walmart v. Actium Co., 400 S.W.3d 906 (Tex. App. 2018) (Category 1 hurricane that made landfall 20 hours after the required time for delivery), the court excused the shipper's performance as well.***
>
> *For these reasons and under this line of cases, Defendant's performance should be excused, because Hurricane Chloe constituted a force majeure event.*

Deferring discussion of the later cases does operate as an exception to the principles of keeping related contentions together and of placing legal contentions before factual. But the exception can be defended by considering that the string of cases is not so much teaching the law or demonstrating that a conclusion is sound as it is offering a sanity check for the conclusion. Deferring discussion of factually similar cases to the end of an argument also helps avoid the impression of a slog through a forest of case law. If the judge comes to the discussion of factually similar cases at the end, after all the legal contentions and factual contentions have been established, the discussion may go more quickly. Or, if the judge is already convinced, he can (and will) just skim or skip the discussion. That won't hurt your client at all.

4. Rebuttal Placement

Chapter 5 (The Order of Sentences) explained how to draft responsive paragraphs. But where do these paragraphs go?

In reply (*i.e.*, third-filed) briefs, nearly all the arguments and contentions you lay out will be responsive, so these sorts of judgment calls do not arise much there. But most opposition (*i.e.*, second-filed) briefs will feature a mix of affirmative and responsive material. As a general matter, it is preferable to rebut your adversary's contentions only after you have laid out all your affirmative contentions. As Chapter 5 emphasizes, the judge will be more inclined to credit rebuttals of your adversary's position once she is fully convinced of the correctness of your own.

But here too, this is only a generalization. Sometimes you are better off taking on some of your adversary's contentions immediately after you have laid out your own falling in the same group. For example, if you are advancing interpretive contentions, it may make sense to place a responsive paragraph addressing your adversary's own interpretive contentions before affirmatively stating your precedential or prudential. Or if you affirmatively advance a factual contention, you may want to respond directly to your adversary's contrary factual contention before laying out your other affirmative factual contentions.

Another recurring issue is whether to include responsive paragraphs in an opening brief. If briefing rules do not give you the right to file a reply brief, you must include in your brief rebuttals of all significant contentions you anticipate your adversary will make. In the less challenging and more frequent context in which you are entitled to file a reply, the better view is to save most responsive material for reply. There are many reasons why: word limits; the desire not to give your adversary the chance to say you mischaracterized her argument; or the chance the adversary will omit contentions you think she should advance. But here too, you must use judgment. When you are sure that an adversary's opposition brief will feature a strong contention prominently, it may behoove you to rebut it preemptively. This is especially so with factual contentions. Failing to "take the sting" out of bad facts can impair the credibility of the full rebuttal you will make in your reply brief.

Finally, the distinction between opening and opposition briefs gets turned a bit upside down in appellate briefs. For an appellant's opening brief is, functionally, more like an opposition brief in which you are rebutting arguments the judge made to rule against your client in the judgment or order under appeal. Similarly, an appellee's brief will resemble in some respects an opening brief simply because the appellee's first job is to defend the lower court's ruling by teaching what it held and arguing affirmatively why it was right. Rebutting the appellant's arguments should generally come after you have defended the lower court's ruling affirmatively.

5. IRAC and Related Principles of Argument Organization

By now, many readers may be asking how the principles of argument organization laid out in this chapter correlate with the "Issue–Rule–Application–Conclusion" (IRAC) method taught for decades in law school and bar exam preparation courses. The answer is that the two approaches are broadly consistent with each other. By calling for the writer to teach the reader the *Issue* and the governing *Rule* before *Applying* the *Rule* to the facts, IRAC implements *Teach first–Argue later*. And by calling for discussion of the *Rule* before *Applying* the *Rule* to the facts, IRAC respects the advice to place legal contentions before factual. An elaboration of IRAC, "Conclusion–Rule–Proof-of-Rule–Application–Conclusion" (CRuPAC),[1] was developed to deal with the many settings in which some legal contentions are uncontested and others are contested and thus need to be proved (*e.g.*, the per-bank rule advocated by Bittner in *Bittner v. United States*). CRuPAC too is consistent with TFAL because CRuPAC calls for the writer to teach the reader all uncontested legal contentions (*Rule*) before arguing contested (*Proof-of-Rule*).

But as this chapter has tried to show, IRAC, CRuPAC, and other variants cannot get you over the finish line for organizing the arguments you will encounter in practice. For that, you need to be sensitive to the need to group related contentions together, a topic the acronyms do not address. Nor do these systems, some developed originally as tools for quickly writing exam answers, address the important question of where to place discussions of case law or where to place responsive arguments. For these recurring challenges, the more detailed advice this chapter offers should be more helpful.

* * *

1. Richard K. Neumann, Jr., Legal Reasoning and Legal Writing: Structure, Strategy, and Style § 10.2 (Aspen 5th ed. 2005).

Optimizing the order of paragraphs in an argument calls for rigorous advance work and thinking. Getting the order right calls above all for appreciating that a judge must learn what he needs to know before grappling with the logic of your argument and that his teacher—you, the lawyer—must teach with a calm, confident voice. Once you have taught a judge the background facts and legal principles he needs to know, argument—applying legal contentions to factual to yield conclusions that serve your client—can begin. And that argument, zealous and forceful as it should be, should unfold in a logical fashion, in which related contentions appear together and in which responsive paragraphs generally follow affirmative.

Part Four: The Brief

Chapter 7

The Order of Arguments

Many briefs advance more than one argument, each directed at different claims, distinct elements of liability, separate components of damages, or various issues of evidence or procedure. So the question of how to sequence the various arguments arises. Even though argument sequence appears in this book as the last of the four sequencing challenges brief-writing presents, it is, in practice, the first challenge you will face in drafting a multi-argument brief.

This challenge also tends to be the simplest. Lawyers frequently disagree about the sequence in which arguments should appear, but that is generally because they disagree about how to assess the relative merits of the various arguments the brief presents, not on the sequencing principles. The principles that govern argument sequence are fairly intuitive and commonsensical, and several are based upon professional conventions on which there is general consensus. This chapter will be short.

To determine the sequence of arguments, first assess whether any should appear before others for doctrinal reasons. The clearest examples of such arguments concern subject-matter or appellate jurisdiction. Because courts cannot entertain matters over which they lack such jurisdiction, judges need to assure themselves that their court possesses it before they invest time in reading a brief. Indeed, in federal court at least, this principle takes the form of an obligation on the part of the lawyer to bring to the court's attention jurisdictional defects that may preclude the court from deciding any issue the case presents. For that reason, arguments concerning subject-matter or appellate jurisdiction always appear at the outset of a brief, sometimes in a prefatory jurisdictional statement. For similar reasons, arguments that, though not strictly jurisdictional, address whether the court should entertain a case, appeal, or motion should also appear early. Examples of the latter such arguments are those based on abstention doctrines, the lack of a statutory right of action, non-exhaustion of administrative remedies, federal preemption, and argument waiver. Judges expect to see these sorts of threshold arguments early in a brief (or, in the case of argument waiver, the section of the brief pertaining to the purportedly waived argument). That is their most natural place.

Certain arguments also precede others by convention. It is conventional to present arguments about liability before those concerning damages or penalty and to present arguments about compensatory damages before those concerning punitive damages, interest, or attorneys' fees. It is conventional to discuss (non-jurisdictional) defenses to claims after addressing the elements of the claims themselves. It is conventional to discuss violations or errors that occurred early in a case (*e.g.*, pleading, discovery) before those that occurred later (*e.g.*, trial, post-trial). In addressing several elements of claims, it is conventional to follow the order in which those elements are stated in statutes, cases, or restatements. In patent cases, it is conventional to discuss infringement before validity.

But these are just conventions. You may have briefs in which it makes sense to depart from them. To take a common example, it may make sense to place a particularly impactful and strong damages argument before an argument on liability, to signal that the damages argument deserves special attention. Or you may wish to present an argument challenging a punitive damages award before you challenge the compensatory if the punitive award greatly exceeds the compensatory. It is also common, in writing opposition or reply briefs, to follow the order of arguments your adversary adopted, on the theory that this will simplify side-by-side comparison of the briefs. Perhaps, but there will often be reasons to depart from your adversary's sequence for expositional or rhetorical reasons. If so, you should.

Once you have followed these conventions (or, if appropriate, disregarded them), you then determine how to sequence arguments for which there are not applicable conventions. For example, you may be seeking exclusion of several different witnesses' testimony. You may be seeking dismissal on the basis of several unrelated defenses. Or you may be seeking to preclude three different opinions by a single expert. The conventional advice is to *Lead with your best arguments*. That advice is sound, but to apply it in the real world, it needs some elaboration. You need to know what makes some arguments "better" than others. To do that, you need to assess your arguments according to three parameters: *breadth*, *impact*, and *viability*.

Breadth means the degree to which an argument, if accepted, simplifies the case. If you have two arguments to support a single claim, one of which would establish an element of the claim as a matter of law, the other of which would direct judgment in your favor on the entire claim, then the second argument is broader than the first. If you are seeking to preclude testimony of two experts, one who addresses all issues, the other who addresses only a few, the argument to preclude the testimony of the first expert is broader than the argument to preclude the testimony of the second. If a complaint has four claims and you have two arguments to reject them, one resolving three claims, the other only one, then the first argument is the broader, even if the second argument, if accepted, would help your client more significantly. *In general, place broader arguments before narrower.*

Impact means the degree to which an argument, if credited, will help your client tangibly, either procedurally (*i.e.*, during the litigation) or substantively (*i.e.*, after it ends). So, to return to an example from the last paragraph, an argument that disposes of a single claim that, if upheld, substantially disadvantages your client has more impact than a broader argument that disposes of three collectively less significant claims. An argument to eliminate or support 75 percent of a damages calculation has more impact than an argument targeted at only 50 percent. An argument for reducing a convict's sentence by seven years has more impact than an argument for reducing it by three. In a case in state court, an argument that the federal constitution has been violated has more impact than a claim that the same violation violated only the state's constitution, if only because the first argument creates a potential route to U.S. Supreme Court review. Note that in many contexts, especially remedial, the concepts of breadth and impact converge. *In general, place more impactful arguments before less impactful.*

Viability means an argument's likelihood of success. As between two arguments, one you believe the judge is likely to credit and the other you believe he will probably reject, the first argument is more viable. *In general, place more viable arguments before less viable.*

It is generally clear which arguments are broader or more impactful and which less so. Viability, by contrast, often generates close calls. Lawyers are often themselves unsure of the relative strengths of their arguments; understandably, for law, for better or worse, is not as rigorous a discipline as math. When lawyers collaborating on a brief disagree about the brief's organization, viability is nearly always the turf on which the squabbles occur. But even when the breadth, impact, and viability of your respective arguments are clear, challenges often arise because the arguments you need to present vary along the relevant parameters. A very narrow argument may be very viable; a very impactful argument may be fairly narrow or unlikely to succeed. There are several permutations, which can become vexing when you have three or more arguments.

In such situations, general guidance, beyond what has already been offered, is not helpful. Other factors, such as the historical or procedural sequence in which the issues arose or the numerical sequence of the counts or claims to which the arguments relate, may help organize the brief. Or it may just be easier or more elegant to have some arguments appear before others. If no other reason for ordering arguments presents itself, place simpler arguments before more complex on the theory that, all else being equal, simpler arguments are more viable.

But to illustrate how to apply all these principles, this example may be helpful:

Imagine that you are writing a brief for a client appealing from a federal criminal conviction after a jury trial. At trial, the client was convicted on two felony counts, the first carrying a maximum sentence of five years (the "less serious count"), the second carrying a maximum sentence of 20 years (the "more serious count"), and he was sentenced consecutively on those counts to 25 years of imprisonment. You have identified the following six grounds for appeal:

1. **Duplicitous Count:** The indictment alleged two distinct crimes in the less serious count, rendering that count duplicitous.
2. **Sixth Amendment Violation:** The jury heard hearsay testimony whose admission violated the client's right to confront the witnesses against him.

3. ***Daubert* Error:** An expert witness's testimony was inadmissible under Federal Rule of Evidence 702 because her methodology was not reliable.

4. **Instructional Error:** The judge inaccurately instructed the jury on the elements of the more serious count.

5. **Sentencing Guideline Error:** The judge misunderstood a federal Sentencing Guideline in imposing the maximum sentence for the conviction on the less serious count.

6. **Eighth Amendment Violation:** The imposition of the maximum, 20-year sentence on the more serious count violated the Eighth Amendment's prohibition of cruel and unusual punishment.

To arrive at the optimal sequencing of these arguments, consider first the order conventions would dictate if the arguments were all equally broad, impactful, and viable. On that assumption, the conventional order for the arguments would be to follow the chronological order of the proceedings. That is the order the preceding sequence follows. The less serious count was duplicitous before any witness testified; the fact witness testified before the expert witness; and both witnesses testified before the defendant-appellant was sentenced. Convention also would dictate addressing sentencing errors in the order in which the affected counts appear in the indictment. Thus, the Sentencing Guideline error affecting the first count would appear before the Eighth Amendment violation affecting the second count.

But now see how that initial, conventional sequence will change if the breadth, impact, and viability of the arguments differ, as they clearly do.

Breadth: Of the six arguments, the second and third are the broadest, because they are the only arguments that, if credited, would invalidate the convictions on both counts. The first and fourth would affect the convictions on only one count, so they are less broad. And the two sentencing errors would not affect the conviction on either count; the latter sentencing errors would lead, at most, to resentencing. So consideration of the arguments' relative breadth would lead you to reorder them thus:

2. Sixth Amendment Violation (Both Counts)

3. *Daubert* Error (Both Counts)

1. Duplicitous Count (Less Serious Count)

4. Instructional Error (More Serious Count)

5. Sentencing Guideline Error (Less Serious Count)

6. Eighth Amendment Violation (More Serious Count)

Impact: Now consider the arguments' respective impacts. The second and third arguments (now appearing in the lead positions) are also the most impactful and equally so because, if credited, each individually invalidates the convictions on both counts. So they should remain the lead arguments. But the order of the duplicitous count error and the instructional error (now appearing third and fourth) should be flipped. The instructional error should precede the duplicitous count error because the instructional error infects the conviction on the more serious count. As between the two final, sentencing errors, the Eighth Amendment violation, which affects the 20-year sentence, is clearly more impactful than the Sentencing Guideline error because the latter affects the five-year sentence only. So the order of these two arguments should be flipped too.

The resulting order is now:

2. Sixth Amendment Violation (Both Counts)

3. *Daubert* Error (Both Counts)

4. Instructional Error (More Serious Count)

1. Duplicitous Count (Less Serious Count)

6. Eighth Amendment Violation (More Serious Count)

5. Sentencing Guideline Error (Less Serious Count)

Viability: Finally, consider how the relative strengths of the arguments affect their order. Here you will have to use judgment, based on your knowledge of the law and, to a lesser extent, the leanings of the appellate court in which the appeal will be heard. (And in criminal appeals you will have to be sensitive to presenting all grounds for appeal, not just some, to avoid a later charge of ineffective assistance of appellate counsel.) But assume for this exercise that of the six grounds for appeal, two are likely to prevail, two are unlikely to prevail, and two are toss-ups. Now things can start to get tricky and open to reasonable disagreement.

If the Eighth Amendment violation is unlikely to prevail, while the Sentencing Guideline error is strong, that probably warrants flipping the order of the last two arguments. Similarly, if the *Daubert* error is strong but the Sixth Amendment violation is probably a loser, that favors flipping the order of the first two arguments. If the duplicitous count error and the instructional error are toss-ups, that probably counsels in favor of leaving their order alone.

So that yields this final sequence of arguments:

3. ***Daubert* Error (Both Counts)**

2. **Sixth Amendment Violation (Both Counts)**

4. **Instructional Error (More Serious Count)**

1. **Duplicitous Count (Less Serious Count)**

5. **Sentencing Guideline Error (Less Serious Count)**

6. **Eighth Amendment Violation (More Serious Count)**

As this exercise shows, assessing the arguments' relative breadth, impact, and viability leads to meaningful departures from the initial, purely chronological ordering.

Most lawyers will not choose to adopt this algorithmic approach to ordering arguments. Most will just pick a sequence and then modify it recursively until it seems just right. That makes sense. For most briefs, the rigor of the foregoing exercise is overkill. And for many, close calls about the relative viability of the arguments may make the exercise falsely precise. But the process illustrated here can educate your intuition. It can also, in planning a complex brief, help you consider sequencing options you might otherwise overlook.

* * *

The order of arguments generally presents itself as the first sequencing challenge you must meet. It is also generally the easiest so long as all the lawyers submitting a brief assess the various arguments similarly.

In sequencing arguments, you should be sensitive to several conventions that apply to argument sequencing. When those conventions do not apply or when they are appropriately disregarded, the relative breadth, impact, and viability of the various arguments should guide their sequencing.

Chapter 8

The Table of Contents

As the first page of every brief, the table of contents is where your arguments make their first impression. With its bird's-eye view of those arguments, the table provides, according to many judges, a better sense of a brief's strengths and weaknesses than the introduction or preliminary statement many briefs contain. As between a well-written table of contents and a well-written introduction, one could argue that the first is a more important unit of advocacy.

Because the table of contents will be the first thing the judge reads, the goal should be to write it in a way that primes her to understand everything that follows. To that end, a table of contents should not only summarize crisply the brief's arguments but also achieve two other objectives. It should

- help the judge form a mental image of the decision tree she will use in deciding the case; and
- introduce the judge gently, without detail, to the factual context of the dispute.

This chapter will offer some techniques and tips for accomplishing both goals.

A. Depicting the Decision Tree

As the metaphor of a decision tree implies, the branching structure of the table of contents is perfect for depicting with text the logical flowchart judges and lawyers see with their mind's eye when they think about a dispute on a high level. You should exploit this unique, non-linear feature of the table of contents to the fullest extent.

To underscore this point, consider this hypothetical table of contents from a brief in support of a motion seeking judgment as a matter of law (JMOL) or a new trial in an antitrust action:

I. JMOL Should Be Entered Because Plaintiff Lacks Antitrust Standing.

II. JMOL Should Be Entered Because Plaintiff Was Not a Direct Purchaser of the Goods Produced by Defendants.

III. JMOL Should Be Entered Because Plaintiff Did Not Suffer Injury by Reason of the Antitrust Laws.

IV. JMOL Should Be Entered Because, in Violation of Fed. R. Evid. 702, the Expert Lacked Expertise Relevant to the Opinions He Offered.

V. JMOL Should Be Entered Because, in Violation of Fed. R. Evid. 702, Plaintiff's Expert's Opinions Were Not Based Upon the Exercise of a Reliable Methodology.

VI. A New Trial Should Be Held Because Plaintiff Elicited Highly Prejudicial Testimony About a Prior Antitrust Settlement.

VII. A New Trial Should Be Held Because the Closing Argument of Plaintiff's Attorney Referred to Highly Prejudicial Evidence Excluded at Trial.

VIII. JMOL Should Be Entered Because the Damage Award Was Not Supported by the Testimony of Plaintiff's Damages Expert.

IX. The Court Should Order a Remittitur of 75% of the Damage Award Because the Award Was Four Times Higher Than the Damages Calculation Proffered by Plaintiff's Damages Expert.

Such a table gives the judge an overview of the nine arguments that will follow. But that is about it. The arguments' logical architecture is obscured by the table's simple structure as a list. Once the table is revised to appear in the conventional format, the various paths to a decision the judge can take start to appear:

I. JMOL Should Be Entered Because Plaintiff Lacks Antitrust Standing.

A. Plaintiff Was Not a Direct Purchaser of the Goods Produced by Defendants.

B. Plaintiff Did Not Suffer Injury by Reason of the Antitrust Laws.

II. JMOL Should Be Entered Because Plaintiff's Expert's Opinions Offended Fed. R. Evid. 702.

A. Plaintiff's Expert Lacked Expertise Relevant to the Opinions He Offered.

B. Plaintiff's Expert's Opinions Were Not Based Upon the Exercise of a Reliable Methodology.

III. A New Trial Should Be Held Because the Court Allowed the Jury to Consider Highly Prejudicial Evidence and Argument.

A. Plaintiff Elicited Highly Prejudicial Testimony About a Prior Antitrust Settlement.

B. The Closing Argument of Plaintiff's Attorney Referred to Highly Prejudicial Evidence Excluded at Trial.

IV. The Damage Award Should Be Vacated.

A. JMOL Should Be Entered Because the Damage Award Was Not Supported by the Testimony of Plaintiff's Damages Expert.

B. The Court Should Order a Remittitur of 75% of the Damage Award Because the Award Was Four Times Higher Than the Damages Calculation Proffered by Plaintiff's Damages Expert.

A judge reviewing the revised table with its branching format will appreciate that what first appears dauntingly as a set of nine arguments is in fact more like four, each of which has two alternative arguments. The judge will also come to appreciate quickly that if he decides I or II in the movant's favor, he need not reach III or IV; or that if he decides III.A in the movant's favor, he will not have to address III.B. He will understand that he reaches IV only if he decides I–III against the movant. He will understand that I.A and I.B both assert defenses that fall under the rubric of antitrust standing. Etc. Having this mental map in place before reading the brief is helpful.

Here is another example of a table of contents that both gives a good overview of the arguments and illustrates the relevant decision tree:

I. *The Doctrine of Assignor Estoppel Should Continue to Be Recognized.*

   A. *Congress Incorporated Assignor Estoppel into the Patent Act.*

   B. *This Court Has Interpreted the Patent Act to Include Assignor Estoppel.*

II. *The Doctrine of Assignor Estoppel Should Not Be Narrowed.*

   A. *Assignor Estoppel May Be Asserted Against Not Only Assignors of Patents but Also Assignors of Patent Applications.*

   B. *Assignor Estoppel May Be Invoked to Bar Challenges to Invalidity Under § 112.*

Even if the judge does not know anything about the obscure patent law doctrine of assignor estoppel, he can nonetheless glean from the table of contents that that doctrine defeats at least some defenses asserted by those who made some sort of assignment earlier. That eases the judge into the more detailed discussion of the doctrine the brief will offer.

Of course, most briefs feature hierarchically organized tables of contents, but the entries often have asymmetries or clutter that can cloud the arguments' relationships. Consider the following very simple table of contents from a motion to dismiss a complaint:

I. *The Complaint Should Be Dismissed Because It Does Not Comply With F.R.C.P. 12.*

   A. *The Complaint Does Not Plausibly Allege That the Bank's Conduct Proximately Caused the Attacks.*

   B. *The Complaint Fails to Plausibly Allege That the Bank Engaged in an Act of International Terrorism.*

This table effectively indicates that the movant is seeking dismissal on two grounds and that both assert that the complaint's allegations are implausible. But the slightly different phrasings of I.A and I.B obscure the similarity and equivalent force of each ground. The following revision makes these symmetries clearer:

> *I. The Complaint Should Be Dismissed Because It Does Not Comply With F.R.C.P. 12.*
>
> *A. The Complaint Does Not Plausibly Allege That the Bank Proximately Caused the Attacks.*
>
> *B. The Complaint Does Not Plausibly Allege That the Bank Engaged in an Act of International Terrorism.*

Sometimes you can clarify the symmetries by simply moving the most important idea in each entry's sentence to the end. If you move the adverbs in each of the second-level entries of the following table to the end of each sentence, you will signal that both arguments focus on the judgment contemnor's intent. Compare:

> *I. The Lower Court Erred in Finding That Harris Had Violated the Judgment With the Requisite Intent.*
>
> *A. The Lower Court Erred in Finding That Harris Had* ***Willfully*** *Violated the Judgment.*
>
> *B. The Lower Court Erred in Finding That Harris Had* ***Inexcusably*** *Violated the Judgment.*

with:

> *I. The Lower Court Erred in Finding That Harris Had Violated the Judgment With the Requisite Intent.*
>
> *A. The Lower Court Erred in Finding That Harris Had Violated the Judgment* ***Willfully****.*
>
> *B. The Lower Court Erred in Finding That Harris Had Violated the Judgment* ***Inexcusably****.*

You will also clarify the only difference between the two arguments. Entries that use parallel constructions and word placements to emphasize similarities and differences enable the judge to read the table of contents as an x-ray of the brief's logic.

Making entries crisper also helps the table of contents perform this job. It is harder to take in a table like this:

I. *Petitioner's CSA and CSA-Dependent Convictions Should Be Reversed Because a Physician Authorized to Prescribe Controlled Substances May Not Be Convicted Unless She Acts Without a "Good-Faith Medical Purpose."*

   A. *The CSA's Text, Structure and History Show That Physicians Must Be Permitted to Assert a Defense of "Good-Faith Medical Purpose."*

   B. *The "Good-Faith Medical Purpose" Standard Accords with the Subjective Good-Faith Standard Adopted by the First, Seventh, and Ninth Circuits.*

   C. *At a Bare Minimum, Any Objective Good-Faith Standard Must Afford Physicians Breathing Room for Honest Departures from Professional Norms.*

II. *Even Under an Objective Good-Faith Standard—Indeed, Under Any Circuit's Law but the Eleventh's—Petitioner's Convictions Should Be Reversed.*

than a table like this:

I. *The CSA Does Not Authorize Conviction If the Physician Acted in Good Faith.*

   A. *The CSA Recognizes the Defense of "Good-Faith Medical Purpose."*

   B. *Three Circuit Courts Have Recognized the Defense of "Good-Faith Medical Purpose."*

   C. *Alternatively, Any Objective Standard Must Afford Physicians More Latitude Than the Standard Under Which Petitioner Was Convicted.*

II. *Even Under the Objective Standard Applied by the Court of Appeals, Petitioner's Convictions Should Be Reversed.*

The second, shorter version is probably better even if the rhetorical force of the first is, for some readers, more powerful.

Brevity is especially important in drafting table of contents entries because their block-indented, single-spaced text makes them harder to read than textual sentences. The entries, even when deeply indented, should never on brief paper exceed four lines of text, preferably fewer. And apropos of formatting, do not use all caps for entries or their associated textual headings.[1] All caps are unnatural and imply agitation. For high-level entries (I, A), use initial caps instead; for lower-level (1, a), capitalize as you would a textual sentence.

Once you have a good structure for the table of contents, the next step is to improve each entry to make the structure and content of the arguments even clearer. A few pointers beyond those offered in Chapters 2 through 4 (Part 1, The Sentence) apply specially to table of contents entries:

1. State the Reason for Each Result.

To permit the table of contents to serve as a summary of the arguments, it is often useful, space permitting, for the table's entries to contain a succinct statement why an argument should prevail. You typically do this using the word '*because*.'

> *The claim for trespass should be dismissed* ***because*** *Plaintiff has not alleged causation.*
>
> *Dr. Wang's expert testimony should be admitted* ***because*** *his opinions are based on a reliable method.*
>
> *Harrison's testimony should not be credited* ***because*** *she was not present at the site of the murder.*

are better than:

> *The claim for trespass should be dismissed.*
>
> *Dr. Wang's expert testimony should be admitted.*
>
> *Harrison's testimony should not be credited.*

Even though the second examples are shorter, the first are better because they allow the judge to get a sense of the arguments' content. In drafting such because-clauses, the challenge is to make them succinct. If that challenge can be met, they are preferable.

A reason not to include because-clauses exists when an entry signifies the grouping of several related arguments or contentions.

---

1. *See* SEVENTH CIRCUIT PRACTITIONER'S HANDBOOK FOR APPEALS 176 (2020).

Such a grouping entry should simply state the desired result, with the several reasons for the result appearing in the subordinate entries:

> ***I. The Claim for Trespass Should Be Dismissed.***
>
> A. *The Claim for Trespass Should Be Dismissed Because Plaintiff Has Not Alleged Causation.*
>
> B. *The Claim for Trespass Should Be Dismissed Because Plaintiff Has Not Alleged That He Owned the Property.*
>
> C. *The Claim for Trespass Should Be Dismissed Because Plaintiff Has Not Alleged That He Suffered Any Compensable Injury.*

Although the first-level entry could have included a because-clause, the resulting entry, articulating each of the three bases for dismissal, would have become so long as to be unwieldy. In that common situation, the higher-level, "headline" entry should omit a statement of reasons, while the subordinate entries should state them individually.

There are also contexts in which a subordinate entry can merely state the reason without a preceding '*because*':

> *I. The Claim for Trespass Should Be Dismissed.*
>
> A. *Plaintiff Has Not Alleged Causation.*
>
> B. *Plaintiff Has Not Alleged That He Owned the Property.*
>
> C. *Plaintiff Has Not Alleged That He Suffered Any Compensable Injury.*

Even though '*because*' does not appear in the three subordinate entries, their placement under the primary entry, together with their similar syntax (see next paragraph), allows the preliminary '*The Claim for Trespass Should Be Dismissed Because . . . .*' to be omitted. This abbreviated approach can be necessary when entries would become too long without the compression. Otherwise, it is a matter of taste.

2. When Possible, Describe Parallel Arguments with Similar Syntax.

Note that in the two preceding examples, entries on the same level have a similar syntax. In the first, all three subordinate entries take the form '*The Claim for Trespass Should Be Dismissed Because Plaintiff Has Not Alleged . . . .*' In the second, they all begin '*Plaintiff*

Has Not Alleged . . . .' This parallelism is deliberate. A less careful drafter might have drafted the entries as follows:

> I. *The Claim for Trespass Should Be Dismissed.*
>
> > A. *The Court Should Dismiss the Trespass Claim Because Plaintiff Has Not Alleged Causation.*
> >
> > B. *The Trespass Claim Should Be Dismissed Because Plaintiff Did Not Own the Property.*
> >
> > C. *Compensable Injury Has Not Been Alleged.*

Each of these entries is fine as a standalone argument heading. But when they appear as vertically stacked table of contents entries, their different sentence structures obscure the relationships among the three arguments. The judge should be able to see from the way in which the three subordinate entries are articulated that Argument I consists of three independent bases for dismissal, each based on the plaintiff's failure to allege an essential element of his claim (causation, standing, and injury). Parallel syntax helps the judge see that.

3. Use the Passive Voice to Show Similarities or Differences.

In the foregoing examples, many of the entries have been cast in the passive voice. That choice was not inevitable. One of the exemplary tables could have read as follows:

> I. *The Court Should Dismiss the Claim for Trespass.*
>
> > A. *The Court Should Dismiss the Claim for Trespass Because Plaintiff Has Not Alleged Causation.*
> >
> > B. *The Court Should Dismiss the Claim for Trespass Because Plaintiff Has Not Alleged That He Owned the Property.*
> >
> > C. *The Court Should Dismiss the Claim for Trespass Because Plaintiff Has Not Alleged That He Suffered Any Compensable Injury.*

These are good sentences. Each could appear in the text of the argument and, actively voiced as all are, would probably be better than their passively voiced counterparts. But in a table of contents, the passively voiced entries are superior:

I. *The Claim for Trespass Should Be Dismissed.*

A. *The Claim for Trespass Should Be Dismissed Because Plaintiff Has Not Alleged Causation.*

B. *The Claim for Trespass Should Be Dismissed Because Plaintiff Has Not Alleged That He Owned the Property.*

C. *The Claim for Trespass Should Be Dismissed Because Plaintiff Has Not Alleged That He Suffered Any Compensable Injury.*

By casting the entries in the passive voice ('*The Claim for Trespass Should* ***Be Dismissed*** . . . .'), you allow the judge, reading quickly and vertically, to see immediately the topic of the headed argument: '*The Claim for Trespass*,' as opposed to some other claim. Since a goal of the table of contents is to show relationships between arguments, pushing that topic to the front of each indented entry serves that purpose better than burying it in the middle.

Just as the passive voice can help show the unity of related arguments, so too it can put a spotlight on their relevant differences:

I. *The Court Should Dismiss the Action.*

A. *The Court Should Abstain Because the Action Presents a Political Question.*

B. *The Court Should Not Entertain the Action Because Its Claims* ***Are Federally Preempted****.*

C. *The Court Should Dismiss the Action Because Its Claims* ***Were Previously Adjudicated****.*

By using the passive voice in entries B ('. . . *Are Federally Preempted*') and C ('. . . *Were Previously Adjudicated*'), you can place at the end of each the words that distinguish the three grounds for decision. In the context of a table of contents, these distinctions are the most important ideas to emphasize. Placing the words that make these distinctions at the end of each sentence gives them that emphasis.

Nearly every table of contents entry articulated as a full sentence will present a choice between the active and passive voice. Make that choice thoughtfully, mindful of the special purposes the table of contents serves.

4. Use '*Should*,' Not '*Must*.'

In this chapter's examples, the entries have, in describing the requested judicial action, used the word '*should*' rather than '*must*.' Compare:

> I. *The Court* **Should** *Dismiss the Action.*
>
> A. *The Court* **Should** *Abstain Because the Action Presents a Political Question.*
>
> B. *The Court* **Should** *Not Entertain the Action Because Its Claims Are Federally Preempted.*
>
> C. *The Court* **Should** *Dismiss the Action Because Its Claims Were Previously Adjudicated.*

with:

> I. *The Court* **Must** *Dismiss the Action.*
>
> A. *The Court* **Must** *Abstain Because the Action Presents a Political Question.*
>
> B. *The Court* **Must** *Not Entertain the Action Because Its Claims Are Federally Preempted.*
>
> C. *The Court* **Must** *Dismiss the Action Because Its Claims Were Previously Adjudicated.*

Even though '*must*' is more legally accurate when referring (as here) to non-discretionary grounds for dismissal, using it here would be a subtle psychological mistake. No one likes to be told they *must* do something even when it's true. Treat the judge with the deference afforded to all powerful individuals with free will. Use '*should*' instead of '*must*,' and then make your arguments so powerful that the judge would rule for your client even if the mandatory determination were discretionary.

5. Avoid Compound Entries.

Inherent in the notion of an outline is that each major entry should state a single argument. Those arguments will often have sub-arguments, but the outline works best in depicting the decision tree if individual subarguments occupy their own individual subordinate levels.

It follows that compound entries like these are poor:

- *Plaintiff Waived Any Argument That Defendant Consented to Jurisdiction, and That Argument Is Meritless in Any Event.*
- *The Use of a Screen Violated the Defendant's Confrontation Right, and the Court's Erroneous Use of the Screen Was Not Harmless.*
- *The Trial Court Properly Declined to Instruct the Jury on Manslaughter; Alternatively, Any Error in Omitting the Instruction Was Harmless.*
- *The Executive Order Removing the County Prosecutor Does Not Allege Violation of Any Statutory Duty, and the County Prosecutor Has No Duty to Follow the Policies of the Governor.*

Compound sentences like these have their place in the text of a brief, especially in textual summaries of argument. But in a table of contents they obscure the branches of the arguments' logic. Thus, they undermine one of the unique strengths of such tables.

There are two ways to revise a compound entry. The first is to recast the entire entry—e.g., '*Plaintiff Waived Any Argument That Defendant Consented to Jurisdiction, and That Argument Is Meritless in Any Event*'—as a single, more general entry:

- *Defendant Did Not Consent to Jurisdiction.*

The second is to break up the entry—e.g., '*The Trial Court Properly Declined to Instruct the Jury on Manslaughter; Alternatively, Any Error in Omitting the Instruction Was Harmless*'—into two entries:

A. *The Trial Court Properly Declined to Instruct the Jury on Manslaughter.*

B. *Any Error in Omitting the Instruction Was Harmless.*

Sometimes it's best to combine the two approaches:

I. *The County Prosecutor Should Be Reinstated.*

A. *The Executive Order Removing the County Prosecutor Does Not Allege Violation of Any Statutory Duty.*

> B. *The County Prosecutor Has No Duty to Follow the Policies of the Governor.*

Use whichever approach works best in light of the overall structure of your argument.

B. Introducing Factual Context

In addition to summarizing the brief's arguments, the table of contents can also ease the judge into the facts of the dispute. To be sure, the table of contents is not the place to try to narrate facts or the procedural history of the dispute; that is the role of background statements. But the table of contents can usefully begin to familiarize the judge with the dispute's who, what, when, and where. That not only makes the ensuing background statements marginally easier to follow but also, perhaps more importantly, makes abstract, clinical argument entries more vivid and concrete. There are two ways to achieve both objectives.

1. Include Allusions to Facts.

You can sometimes work into the entries allusions to the setting in which the dispute arose or to provisions governing the dispute. So long as the allusion does not unduly lengthen the entry and does not repeat information in prior entries, the allusion is generally helpful. Consider the following excerpt from the table of contents in an insurance coverage dispute:

> I. *The Invoked Exclusions Do Not Preclude Coverage.*
>
> A. *The Wear-and-Tear Exclusion Does Not Preclude Coverage.*
>
> B. *The Faulty-Workmanship Exclusion Does Not Preclude Coverage.*

The entries become a bit more inviting when they allude to the nature of the claim for coverage and of the exclusions that lie at the core of the dispute:

> I. *The Invoked Exclusions Do Not Preclude Coverage for Damages Resulting from the Release of 90 Tons of Liquefied Chlorine from Burlington's Tank Car.*

> A. *The Wear-and-Tear Exclusion Does Not Preclude Coverage Because the Tank Car's Crack Did Not Result from a Gradual Degradative Process.*
>
> B. *The Faulty-Workmanship Exclusion Does Not Preclude Coverage Because the Cause of the Tank Car's Crack Is Unknown.*

The pithiness of the original entries is a plus, but the increased informational content of the contextualized entries justifies their moderately greater length.

Here is another example from a brief concerning class certification:

> I. *The District Court Did Not Abuse Its Discretion in Certifying a Class.*
>
> A. *The District Court Applied the Proper Standard for Assessing Whether Defendant Unlawfully Exercised Monopsony Power.*
>
> B. *The District Court Properly Certified a Liability Class.*
>
> II. *The District Court Properly Followed In re Polypropylene Antitrust Litig.*

Seasoning the entries with some context is helpful even though it lengthens them modestly:

> I. *The District Court Did Not Abuse Its Discretion in Certifying a Class of Oil and Gas Lessors in Eastern Laramie County.*
>
> A. *The District Court Applied the Proper Standard for Assessing Whether Defendant, Through Its Capture Program, Unlawfully Exercised Monopsony Power.*
>
> B. *The District Court Properly Certified a Liability Class of Lessors Who Were Unable to Lease Their Oil and Gas Fields Owing to Defendant's Capture Program.*
>
> II. *The District Court Properly Followed In re Polypropylene Antitrust Litigation's Dispensation from Proof of Individual Class Member Impact.*

No judge coming to this case cold will understand from the table of contents what the '*Capture Program*' is or the holding of *In re Polypropylene Antitrust Litigation*. That is okay. The point is to plant in the judge's mind a few seeds from which deeper understanding will emerge a few pages later.

Some lawyers may retort that by the time a judge takes up a class certification motion, she has undoubtedly resolved several motions and is thus already familiar with the case. Perhaps, but even skilled, engaged judges benefit from being reminded of the context of a complex case that is only one of hundreds vying for attention on their docket. And although the judge may already be familiar with the case, her perhaps newly hired clerk will not have the same background to draw upon.

2. Use Descriptive Proper Nouns.

Lawyers steeped in a case like to use numerical proper nouns: *e.g.*, Claim 4, Count III, the '336 Patent, Paragraphs 2–41, Section 4.3. This is understandable. In a complex case, numerical proper nouns are often the most efficient way to discuss the various issues the case presents. But for a newcomer to the case, numbers can exasperate. They communicate nothing about the substance of the enumerated claim, count, allegation, or contract provision. For numerical proper nouns substitute descriptive:

Claim 4 → *The Trespass Claim*

Count III → *The Felon-in-Possession Charge*

The '336 Patent → *The Patent-in-Suit*

Paragraphs 2–41 → *The Reliance Allegations*

Section 4.3 → *The Force Majeure Clause*

Granted, it will be appropriate at least at the outset of background statements and arguments to refer to the referenced claim, count, etc. with its proper number. But consider replacing the numerical proper noun after its first appearance with a more descriptive term, like those just listed. Briefs using descriptive proper nouns are easier to follow.

About the only reason not to de-number the proper nouns in a table of contents is if you are responding to a brief that uses numerical nomenclature. In that common situation, you may prefer to adopt the same nomenclature as the opening brief so that the judge does not have to learn a new system when he turns to your brief. In opening briefs, however, descriptive nomenclature will help make the judge's learning curve a bit less steep.

* * *

The table of contents offers a special opportunity to give the judge an overview of the dispute at precisely the point in the brief—the first page—at which an overview offers its greatest value. A well-set table of contents provides both a high-level view of the architecture of an argument and a helpful diagram of its supporting beams. To help the table play that important role, make the syntax of related entries elucidate the underlying arguments' relationships. And give the entries more vivid force by including, where possible, allusions to the dispute's facts.

Chapter 9

Background Statements

For many years in New York City, a respected trial lawyer ran ads in which he asserted that the secret to winning jury trials is to "make the jury *want* to rule in your favor." Many lawyers would go further: the secret to winning all non-frivolous litigation, jury or non-jury, lower court or appellate, is to instill in the decision-maker—juror, judge, or arbitrator—a personal desire to rule your client's way. Like so much advice about litigation, this advice does not lend itself to objective testing. And in many instances, the advice will be easier to offer than to follow. But you should try to follow it. It is probably sound.

In briefs, the place to follow this advice with special care is the introductory statement that lays out the facts on which the arguments will rely. This statement goes by various names: Statement of Facts, Background, Procedural History, Statement of the Case, etc. This chapter will refer to all such statements as background statements. Even when briefing rules do not require a background statement, the statement offers a mostly irreplaceable opportunity to align the judge's sympathies with the client's interests. You should seize this opportunity by applying two disciplines: psychology and pedagogy.

Applying psychology means identifying ways to present your client and yourself as likable.

To make your client likable, you identify themes and facts about your client or his case that inspire sympathy. Ideally these will be circumstances and attributes relevant to the legal standard the judge will apply. But even if not relevant to that standard, they are still valuable to describe, if only subtly. When, for example, representing those accused or convicted of crimes, you must find something, modest as it may be, that can make your client, if not appealing, then at least worthy of some measure of leniency. That is so even in—perhaps especially in—submissions filed before the sentencing phase; for by that phase, the judge's impressions will have hardened. In a patent case, it is nearly always good, if representing the patentholder, to emphasize the problem the inventor solved and how the solution contributed to human welfare, even if the submission concerns an issue to which the novelty of the invention is not germane.

Exceptions to this principle exist. In briefs concerning purely procedural issues, it is often effective to keep the submission as clinical as possible. But even in such briefs, there will often be facts relating to the procedural posture or history of the case that make your position more subjectively appealing: *e.g.*, the earlier procedural misconduct of your adversary, the good faith of your client in a prior procedural dispute. Working these in at the outset can help you win the judge over to your side.

To make you, the lawyer, likable, the approach is entirely different. You do not provide details about yourself. In legal writing, you, the lawyer, should be totally invisible. Rather, you control what literary critics would call your narrative voice. In social contexts, a likable voice or manner is, depending on the context, casual, witty, self-deprecating, modest, ebullient, cheerful, sarcastic, impassioned, empathic, non-judgmental, etc. In advocacy, a likable voice is none of those things. When writing a background statement, you should aim, like a commercial airline pilot making an announcement during a period of turbulence, to come off as calm, confident, authoritative, and serious. These are the attributes of an individual to whom, in non-social contexts, human beings will want to draw closer. These are the attributes of an individual whom human beings will instinctually trust.

Above all, you should avoid coming off as argumentative. Yes, you are a lawyer. Yes, your job is to argue. But the place for argument is the argument section alone. Judges are more likely to credit arguments after they have first learned the facts from a person they have come to like and trust. People do not like or trust those who come off as argumentative or combative at the outset of a relationship. They especially don't like or trust such people when they express views at odds with their own. Yet judges who are not initially well disposed to your client's positions are precisely the type of people you must aim to win over.

Although the advice to avoid being argumentative runs against the grain of many lawyers, it is surprisingly easy to follow when writing background statements. To avoid argument in this setting, you avoid using overtly critical adjectives, like *egregious*, *blatant*, *purported*, or *bald*. You avoid making statements that are in fact opinions, such as '*it is undisputed that*,' '*adversary's brief contains many misstatements of the record*,' or '*of course*.' You avoid using the ordinal adjectives ('*First*, . . . *Second*, . . .') lawyers use (too often; see Chapter 3, The Persuasive Sentence, at pp. 56–58) when rattling off arguments. You even avoid using fairly neutral terms that nonetheless give the sentence the flavor of a legal conclusion, the very terms you will—and should—use in the ensuing argument sections. So instead of:

> *By selling the product in Kansas, X breached the Agreement.*

write the slightly longer:

> *By selling the product in Kansas, X engaged in conduct the Agreement prohibited.*

Or in the following paragraph from the background statement of a motion to dismiss for lack of personal jurisdiction, consider deleting the last sentence:

> *Mr. Harris does not have any office, bank account, asset, or interest in any property within New Jersey. He has never entered into or performed any contract in New Jersey. Over the course of his entire life, he has visited the United States only on family vacations, and on those, he never traveled to New Jersey other than to board a connecting flight through Newark Airport.* ***He has never transacted business, regularly solicited business, or derived any substantial revenue from goods used or consumed or services rendered in New Jersey.***

for it heavy-handedly echoes the long-arm statute the judge will later apply. Changes like these help to avoid creating the impression that you are trying to force the judge to draw a legal conclusion before she is ready. They make a background statement more effective, even though in an argument section they would diminish the force of the advocacy. Writing a background statement that is argumentative is a common and serious error lawyers, especially experienced lawyers, make. Fortunately, it is very easy to fix.

Applying pedagogy—the second way to get the judge to like you and your client—means drafting the background statement so that it functions as an instructional text. Pedagogical efficiency will endear you and your client to a judge simply because people like people who help them perform a difficult job. Like the lion with a thorn in his paw, the judge will come to see you as his Androcles if you can provide him with a succinct, but complete, exposition of what he needs to know. Here, a writing text can offer help.

In keeping with this book's overall approach, this chapter will now take up in the context of background statements the four sequencing challenges of legal writing.

A. The Order of Words in a Sentence

If you have learned how to make sentences efficient and professional (the focus of Chapters 2 and 4), you do not need to learn anything else to draft sentences in a background statement. The reasons to keep related words together; to use pronouns unambiguously; to eliminate unnecessary words and to add necessary; to use parallel constructions; and to keep the diction professional apply fully to sentences in background statements.

The advice to put the most important idea at the end of the sentence (a focus of Chapter 3) also applies to sentences in background statements. Here, however, the goal is not to persuade but to educate. For that reason, it is useful to recast the advice. In background statements, the most important idea is likely to be the idea that supplies new information. So try to put that new idea at the end. Its novelty alone will tend to make it the sentence's most important, impactful idea.

For example, the following paragraph:

> *Epilepsy is a debilitating neurological condition that affects approximately 1% of all Americans. Lamotrigine is approved to treat epilepsy.*

should be revised to:

> *Epilepsy is a debilitating neurological condition that affects approximately 1% of all Americans. One of the drugs approved to treat epilepsy is lamotrigine.*

By the time the judge reaches the second sentence, she knows what epilepsy is; she learned about it in the first sentence. The new idea in the second sentence is '*lamotrigine*.' That idea belongs at the end.

Or consider the following excerpt from a procedural history:

> *On May 15, 2022, the appellee filed a petition for rehearing. The court issued a revised opinion after the appellee filed its petition.*

The second sentence should be revised to:

> *After the appellee filed its petition, the court issued a revised opinion.*

because the new idea in that sentence—the only idea that does not appear in the preceding sentence—is the '*revised opinion*.'

For other examples, see Chapter 3, The Persuasive Sentence, at pp. 42–43.

B. The Order of Sentences in a Paragraph

Ordering sentences in the paragraphs of background statements is straightforward. Unlike legal argument, which is a learned, non-intuitive mode of discourse, narration and explanation are fairly natural. A paragraph in a statement of facts will consist of a series of sentences narrating events chronologically, interspersed as appropriate with sentences offering details about those events. Alternatively, and to vary sentence length, you can place the details in clauses or phrases that are part of the narrative sentence itself.

This sounds more complicated than it is. In the following example of a background statement, the purely narrative sentences and clauses appear in bold. You can confirm that by reading them alone. The resulting abridgement, though choppy, nonetheless lays out a coherent chronology of events. In contrast with the narrative material appearing in bold type, the material in normal type offers details about the narrated events.

> ***Charles Hu**, a native of Hong Kong and a naturalized U.S. citizen, **served in the Foreign Service between 1953 and 1978. When he retired in 1978, Hu***

started receiving retirement benefits from the State Department's Foreign Service Retirement and Disability System ("FSRDS"). After he died in 1984, *his wife,* **Leonore Hu, began receiving those benefits as a "survivor annuitant."** *These payments went directly to Leonore Hu's account at First Hawaiian Bank.*

In 1995, Leonore added *her daughter,* **Cheryl Hu, to the account as a co-owner. After Leonore died in 1997, the State Department continued to deposit Leonore's survivor annuity benefits into this account every month, until in 2011, it** *realized the error and* **stopped making the payments***.*

In May 2012, the State Department sent Cheryl a letter *informing her that it had mistakenly deposited $254,000 into her mother's account and that she had to return the funds.* **Next month, Cheryl's counsel sent a letter to the State Department** *requesting that repayment be excused in accord with 22 C.F.R. § 17.2, because "the alleged overpayment is not the result of Cheryl's acts or omission and she is therefore without fault." 22 C.F.R. § 17.2. Section 17.2 provides that "recovery of an overpayment . . . may be waived pursuant to [22 U.S.C. § 4047(d)] when the individual is without fault and recovery would be against equity and good conscience or administratively infeasible."* **Nearly two years later, the State Department responded to Cheryl's letter***, informing her that the amount overpaid was in fact $312,000, and that it could not accommodate her request because "the Department is prohibited from waiving collection of an overpayment to an estate under 22 C.F.R. § 17.7(a)(2)." Section 17.7(a)(2) states that "waiver of an overpayment cannot be granted when . . . the overpayment was made to an estate."* **Cheryl then, in July 2014, appealed the State Department's determination to the Foreign Service Grievance Board***, primarily arguing that she was eligible to seek a waiver because the annuity payments had been deposited directly into her own bank account and not into an account associated with her mother's estate.*

To enhance the flow of background statements, you use many of the same techniques this book described earlier. Making the beginnings of sentences harken back to something at the end of the preceding sentence ("lookback"; see Chapter 3, The Persuasive Sentence, at pp. 51–52) works as well for narrative as for argument. The four lookback applications in the preceding example appear below in bold:

> *Charles Hu, a native of Hong Kong and a naturalized U.S. citizen, served in the Foreign Service between 1953 and* ***1978. When he retired in 1978****, Hu started receiving retirement benefits from the State Department's Foreign Service Retirement and Disability System ("FSRDS"). After he died in 1984, his wife, Leonore Hu, began receiving those benefits as* ***a "survivor annuitant." Her survivor annuitant payments*** *went directly to her account at First Hawaiian Bank.*
>
> *[. . .]*
>
> *In May 2012, the State Department sent Cheryl a letter informing her that it had mistakenly deposited $254,000 into her mother's account and that she had to return the funds. Next month, Cheryl's counsel sent a letter to the State Department requesting that repayment be excused because* ***"the alleged overpayment is not the result of Cheryl's acts or omission and she is therefore without fault." 22 C.F.R. § 17.2. Section 17.2*** *provides that "recovery of an overpayment . . . may be waived pursuant to [22 U.S.C. § 4047(d)] when the individual is without fault and recovery would be against equity and good conscience or administratively infeasible." Nearly two years later, the State Department responded to Cheryl's letter, informing her that the amount overpaid was in fact $312,000, and that it could not accommodate her request because "the Department is prohibited from waiving collection of an overpayment to an estate* ***under 22 C.F.R. § 17.7(a)(2)." Section 17.7(a)(2)*** *states that "waiver of an overpayment cannot be granted when . . . the overpayment was made to an estate." Cheryl then, in July 2014, appealed the State Department's determination to the Foreign Service Grievance Board, primarily arguing that she was eligible to seek a*

> *waiver because the annuity payments had been deposited directly into her own bank account and not into an account associated with her mother's estate.*

In writing background statements, the advice to avoid a series of long or short sentences (see Chapter 5, The Order of Sentences, at pp. 93–94) also applies. But because the ideas in background statements tend to be less complex than the ideas in arguments, the sentences in such statements will naturally tend to be shorter than sentences in argument sections. For that reason, a series of very short sentences may seem less choppy in a background statement than a series of similarly short sentences in an argument section.

One device for enhancing the flow of sentences in arguments that is not as useful when drafting background statements is logical traffic signals (see Chapter 3, The Persuasive Sentence, at pp. 53–56). These should appear less frequently in background statements because they give a narrative a tendentious tone. If you find yourself writing things like *to be sure*, *indeed*, *that said*, *tellingly*, *notably*, or *on the one hand, . . . on the other hand*, in a background statement, that is a telltale sign that you are adopting an argumentative voice.

C. The Order of Paragraphs in a Background Statement

Most background statements, substantive or procedural, are narrative: they recount a series of events. For such statements, the basic mode of organization is nearly always chronological. Although fiction writers and cinematographers can begin works *in medias res* or use flashbacks to moving effect, departing from a strictly chronological approach in a statement of facts or procedural history creates pedagogical risks that the lawyer should not take without a good reason. A statement of facts or procedural history that mechanically ticks off a set of sentences, each beginning '*On Month/Day/Year, . . .*,' in chronological order, will not make for invigorating reading. But from a pedagogical standpoint, it is ahead of the game.

You can moderate some of the monotony of a recitation of dates by adding or substituting phrases that, rather than reciting dates, show relations between them.

> *On May 20, 2021, the court dismissed the complaint.*

becomes:

> *On May 20, 2021,* ***two years after briefing concluded****, the court dismissed the complaint.*

Or:

> *On August 20, 2022 at 4:16 a.m., a Yates County 911 operator received a call from a man who stated that he saw an individual attempting to break into a home in the Rookwater section of Geneva. At 4:30 a.m., police arrived at the home but did not find any individual or any sign of break-in. At 3:30 p.m., an officer retrieved a crowbar lying on the sidewalk. Fingerprint tests performed on August 21 linked the object to Roger Baldwin, a resident of Seneca Falls.*

becomes:

> *On August 20, 2022 at 4:16 a.m., a Yates County 911 operator received a call from a man who stated that he saw an individual attempting to break into a home in the Rookwater section of Geneva.* **A few minutes later***, police arrived at the home but did not find any individual or any sign of break-in.* **Later that day, in the afternoon***, an officer retrieved a crowbar lying on the sidewalk. Fingerprint tests performed* **the next day** *linked the object to Roger Baldwin, a resident of Seneca Falls.*

A special imperative of a statement of facts is stage-setting: introducing persons or legal instruments (e.g., a contract, a patent) with an explicitness that many literary writers abandoned in the modern period. Compare the opening of the biblical *Book of Job*:

> *A man once lived in the land of Utz. His name was Job. This man was innocent, upright, and God-fearing, and kept himself apart from evil. Seven sons and three daughters were born to him. His flock consisted of seven thousand sheep, three thousand camels, five hundred yoke of oxen, five hundred female donkeys, and a large staff of servants. He was the greatest of the men of the East.*[1]

1. The Book of Job 55 (Raymond P. Scheindlin trans., W.W. Norton 1998).

with the opening of Faulkner's *The Sound and the Fury*:

> *Through the fence, between the curling flower spaces, I could see them hitting. They were coming toward where the flag was and I went along the fence. Luster was hunting in the grass by the flower tree. They took the flag out, and they were hitting. Then they put the flag back and they went to the table, and he hit and the other hit, and I went along the fence. Luster came away from the flower tree and we went along the fence and they stopped and we stopped and I looked through the fence while Luster was hunting in the grass.*

In writing narrative background statements, you should emulate the author of *Job*, not Faulkner. That is not because the biblical writer was a better writer than Faulkner. (That is a matter of taste.) It is because Faulkner's careful, deliberate decision to prompt questions in the reader's mind—*Who/what is Luster?*, *Who are they?*, *Who is I?*, *Who is he?*, *Who is the other?*, *What are they hitting?*, *What is the flag?*, and *Where is the fence?*—will only exasperate a judge, even though it will draw the literary reader on.

It is rare to find background statements as obscurantist as the opening of Faulkner's novel or of other great works of modern literature. But you will often find background statements that do not transparently introduce the characters and legal instruments they concern. If, in the first few paragraphs of a narrative, you are not reciting relevant details about the main parties or about the legal instruments pertinent to their dispute, you may be making a mistake.

Consider, for example, the opening paragraph from this statement of facts:

> *Agalma's claims arise from UBT's numerous breaches of the parties' Exclusive Worldwide Licensing Agreement (the "EWLA"), executed on July 13, 2013, as well as from UBT's acts of trademark infringement and its defamation of Agalma. On May 23, 2013, Agalma entered into a confidentiality agreement with UBT before beginning to negotiate the terms of the EWLA. About two months later, on July 13, UBT, Agalma and the other defendants entered into the EWLA. Defendant Morris signed the agreement on behalf of Agalma.*

To better introduce the main characters and agreements, revise it to:

> *Agalma manufactures micro-injection devices under the Agalmatic® trademark. Agalmatic devices employ innovative technology that allows the user to automate the micro-injection process in contexts in which sequential but staggered microinjection is advantageous.*
>
> *On July 13, 2013, Agalma licensed its Agalmatic trademark, as well as the patents covering the technology the Agalmatic devices embody, to UBT. UBT is a publicly traded biotech company, founded by Henry Morris, who now serves as its CEO. Before entering into the July 13, 2013 license agreement, UBT and Agalma entered into a confidentiality agreement to govern the exchange of information during the contemplated license negotiations. Morris then signed the license agreement on behalf of UBT.*

Or consider this opening paragraph from a statement of facts:

> *On March 14, 2022, Abramson filed a Second Amended Complaint setting forth claims of trade dress infringement, unfair competition, and breach of a confidentiality agreement pertaining to MaxCo's improper copying of Abramson's valuable Echo® whiteboard design. On March 28, 2022, Maxco filed an answer and six counterclaims, each of which seeks declaratory relief absolving Maxco of various forms of liability. While Abramson contends that all six of MaxCo's Counterclaims lack merit, Abramson acknowledges that five directly relate to his claims. The first counterclaim, however, has nothing to do with the parties' dispute: it seeks a declaration of non-infringement of a design patent that Abramson has not asserted.*

Revise it to:

> *Based in Fort Worth, Texas, MaxCo is a privately held company that manufactures and sells school and office furniture and accessories. MaxCo and its predecessors have been developing and selling those products for more than thirty years. For the last 15 of those years, MaxCo has sold some of its products in competition with products sold by Defendant Abramson's company, Haskins.*

> *MaxCo started selling its Compass® Porcelain Steel Lapboard in late 2019. When introduced, the Compass lapboard differed from competing lapboards, including those Haskins sells under the Echo® trademark. The lapboard also featured several distinctive features, such as its trapezoidal handle and opening. To protect its investment in developing and marketing its lapboard, MaxCo applied for and obtained a design patent covering these ornamental features.*

Even prosaic stage-setting paragraphs, like the following:

> *Plaintiff ABC Investment, L.P. ("ABC"), is a limited partner in the limited partnership 236 East 6th Street Partnership (the "Partnership"). The other three limited partners are The 1992 Farris Family Trust, The Marcus Family Trust and Jedediah Investments Defined Benefit Plan Trust. The general partner of the Partnership is 417 Spruce Street, Inc. The latter three limited partners and the general partner are the defendants in this action.*
>
> *The Partnership's main asset is an office building in Indianapolis. The Partnership earned rental income from commercial tenants on the first floor and from a hotel located on the upper floors.*
>
> *In 2007, ABC filed this action . . .*

are better than opening paragraphs that 'grab' the judge if those grabbing paragraphs nonetheless raise more questions than they answer.

But you can sometimes set the stage so as to not only identify the protagonists but also grip the judge in a way that might make her want to rule in your client's favor:

> *On June 13, 2017, at 5:58 a.m., Defendant-Appellant, Wendy Hopson, was in bed in the single-wide trailer she shared with her daughter, when Caleb Porter, her former boyfriend, texted her to tell her that she would "end up in a ditch." Wendy texted back at 6:14 a.m. and then again at 6:15 a.m., telling him not to come to her home. At approximately 6:28 a.m., Caleb arrived at her trailer. Enraged, he burst into Wendy's bedroom, grabbed her phone and gun, pointed the gun in her face and assaulted her.*

> *Wendy was afraid Caleb would seriously injure or kill her and her daughter. Less than two minutes after Caleb had broken into her bedroom, threatening to kill her, Wendy shot Caleb twice. Caleb's autopsy revealed that his blood contained methamphetamine at a level of 1.5.*

Sometimes you may have to postpone introducing certain parties or instruments until after the opening paragraphs. If so, make sure nonetheless that every introduction is as explicit as those appearing above. The need for explicit stage-setting in a background statement exists even if you have already introduced the key protagonists in a preliminary statement. The judge may not come to the background statement with a full appreciation of the facts recounted in the preliminary statement. You should draft background statements on the assumption that the judge has only skimmed the preliminary statement or skipped it altogether.

And to return to a point from the last chapter, even trial court briefs filed years into the litigation should be drafted on the assumption that the judge is new to the case. When filing multiple briefs in a matter on the same day (*e.g.*, in limine motions), consider drafting a single, standalone background statement in one of the briefs and then incorporating it by reference into the other, simultaneously filed submissions. (But be mindful that some judges will view incorporation by reference as a means of circumventing word limits.)

Some background statements do not narrate a series of events but instead explain a body of knowledge with which the judge is not familiar. For these, the guiding principle of organization is not chronological. Rather, you should move from general to specific and from more familiar to less familiar.

Thus, in a case involving a drug that treats serious fungal infections, you might begin a background statement in this way:

> *Of the many microorganisms that can infect a human being fatally, fungi comprise a significant number. Although less common than bacterial or viral infections, fungal infections account for more than 70,000 hospitalizations in the United States annually. Such fungal infections are referred to as systemic, to distinguish them from the more common, less serious topical fungal infections (athlete's foot, ringworm,*

> *etc.) with which most people are familiar. Examples of serious, systemic fungal infections include aspergillosis, candidiasis, and histoplasmosis.*
>
> *In treating systemic fungal infections, a physician can draw on a variety of classes of medications. This case concerns the class of antifungal medications known as azoles. Azoles, so named because they all contain an azole chemical group, were first developed in the 1970s. The first azole to win approval from the FDA for the treatment of systemic fungal infections was ketoconazole. Since the approval of ketoconazole in 1977, several other azoles have won FDA approval. The azole that is the subject of this case is isavuconazole. Isavuconazole was approved in 2015.*

The first paragraph adopts a "more familiar → less familiar" approach to sentence sequencing. The second adopts a "general → specific" approach; it opens with a panoramic shot of a drug class and moves toward a close-up on the drug of interest. The goal of both paragraphs is to gradually but efficiently move the judge's attention from some general subject of which he probably has a general awareness—microbial infections—to the specific subject at hand, of which he probably has none: isavuconazole.

Or in a contract dispute, you might describe the contract and the terms central to the dispute like this:

> *In November 2014, MGT entered into an exclusive license agreement (the "ELA") with a small biotech company called Kainos LLC, whereby MGT licensed certain patents covering certain RNA interference therapies. Through the ELA, MGT granted Kainos an "exclusive, worldwide license to manufacture, use and sell . . . Licensed Products." "Licensed Products" were defined to mean compounds whose "manufacture, use or sale would, but for the license granted herein, infringe in whole or in part" a valid claim of one of the patents identified in a schedule to the ELA. In return for exclusive rights to this technology covered by the scheduled patents, Kainos agreed to make royalty and other payments to MGT.*
>
> *One payment term was based on Kainos's receipt of "Sublicense Revenues." "Sublicense revenues" were defined,*

> *with certain exclusions, as "all consideration received by Kainos in return for the grant of rights to manufacture, use and sell a Licensed Product," as, for example, through a sublicense to a third party. But under Section 2.6 of the ELA, Kainos could sublicense the scheduled patents only if MGT consented to the sublicense.*

This passage does not proceed from more familiar to less familiar; all the concepts are new. Rather, it moves from general—the agreement as a whole—to specific—the terms relevant to the dispute.

Background statements are often a good place to teach the judge about legal or administrative frameworks that are not a staple of the docket. In a case involving a system of federal foreign service pension benefits, you might begin the statement as this brief did:

> *Subchapter VIII of the Foreign Services Act, 22 U.S.C. §§ 4041–4071, authorizes the State Department to administer the Foreign Service Retirement and Disability System (the "FSRDS"). Among the many provisions in this subchapter are those governing who is eligible for annuities from the FSRDS and how those annuities are paid, including when and how they are paid to annuitants' survivors. The subchapter also contains a provision outlining when and how the State Department may recover the overpayment of an annuity. 22 U.S.C. § 4047(d).*

Or in a brief opposing a motion to enforce a subpoena against an administrative agency that rarely appears in the court in which enforcement is sought, you might provide background information about the agency as this brief did:

> *The International Trade Commission ("ITC") is a six-member body charged with administering several statutes that regulate imports. Pursuant to Section 337 of the Tariff Act of 1930, 19 U.S.C. § 1337, the ITC investigates allegations of unfair import practices. Such practices include the importation of articles that infringe a United States patent. Id. at § 1337(a)(1)(B)(i). Suspected patent infringement is the impetus for the vast majority of the ITC's Section 337 investigations. Infringements investigated by the ITC often become the subject of infringement actions filed in district court. The ITC is located in the District of Columbia*

> *and does not have satellite offices or any physical presence outside that district.*

Once the background statement, whether narrative or expositional, has gotten off to a good start, finishing it is generally not difficult. Just follow the chronological and other organizational principles described earlier and avoid argument or idiosyncrasy. But a challenge encountered in completing nearly every background statement is how to address bad facts, the facts that every lawyer, no matter how strong his case, wishes he could make disappear. The standard—and correct—answer is that you need to address them in some fashion, ideally before your adversary does. By addressing them preemptively, you not only allow your own explanation for those bad facts to ferment but also subliminally convey to the judge your belief—false as it may be—that these facts are not the case-killers your adversary will portray them to be. (The same advice does not necessarily apply when addressing your adversary's legal arguments. Here, the decision whether to rebut anticipated arguments preemptively is more nuanced. See Chapter 6, The Order of Paragraphs, at pp. 124–125.)

To address bad facts, you should not try to argue them away. Consider a letter brief to a judge seeking an extension of the deadline for completion of fact discovery. As the plaintiff seeking the extension, you should not include in your background statement a passage like this:

> *Defendant will contend that because Plaintiff purportedly delayed its first production, Plaintiff's request now to extend the deadline for fact discovery should not be granted. The first production occurred on April 3, nine months after the complaint was filed, because Defendant failed to cooperate with Plaintiff in drafting a protective order. Once the parties completed the draft order, they submitted it to the Court, and the Court approved it on March 30. Plaintiff made its first production immediately thereafter, belying any inference of dilatory intent on its part.*

Instead, you work the bad facts into your narrative just as you would any other fact, providing favorable details, whatever and however few they may be, neutrally and unemphatically:

> *Between October 15, five weeks after the complaint was filed, and March 30, the parties negotiated a case*

> *management order and a protective order. They completed the first on November 15 and submitted it to the Court for approval immediately thereafter. That case management order was approved on December 10 and, though it called for the substantial completion of document production by June 29, did not set a deadline for the first production. Over the next several months, the parties engaged in somewhat protracted negotiation of the protective order, largely because they disagreed about the number of confidentiality designations. On March 15, they submitted the jointly prepared order to the Court for its approval. Five days after the Court approved the protective order, Plaintiff made its first document production.*

The time for addressing the slow timing of the first production argumentatively will come later.

In briefs filed in the latter part of a case or in an appeal, you frequently have to decide whether to quote testimony from a deposition, trial, or hearing. The impact and credibility of a clean admission of a critical fact are profound. Thus, as a general matter, you should quote testimony and, where helpful, the question that elicited it. A problem, however, arises because many lawyers are not dispassionate judges of the clarity or power of testimony they themselves elicited. They think the admission they won is crisper than it is in fact. Or they try to focus the judge not so much on the content of the testimony as on the fierceness of the battle they fought to win it. (And the fiercer the battle, the more confusing the thrust-and-parry tends to be.) As a result, the background statement devolves into a series of war stories like those so familiar to any lawyer who has had a drink with a colleague who recently tried a case. Unfortunately, this book cannot offer turnkey advice on when to include testimonial excerpts and when to omit them. The best advice it can offer is: *Don't overdo it*.

D. The Order of Background Statements

Briefs that contain only one background statement—most commonly, a statement of facts—are common. Many briefs, however, need to lay out sets of facts that do not naturally fall under a single heading. To evaluate the arguments in a brief, the judge often needs to know both the facts of the case and its procedural history. Those two subjects benefit from separate treatments in a statement of facts and a procedural history. In many civil cases, the facts relevant to damages and liability do not overlap, and you will have to treat them separately. And in appeals from trial judgments, you will need not only to teach the judge the facts in the record but also to describe evidentiary rulings or other rulings during the course of trial or jury selection. Each will have its own body of pertinent facts, and their relation to one another may be fairly distant.

In such submissions, you have two sequencing options:

You can structure all the discussions as subsections of the single background statement that precedes the argument. Typically, you place statements narrating the facts of the case first, followed by procedural histories. This order should be reversed in submissions to courts whose briefing rules require a procedural history to appear first. And in some submissions relating primarily or exclusively to procedural matters, you may appropriately flip the order even if a rule does not require it. In cases in which the non-procedural aspects of the case have several components (*e.g.*, liability, damages, willfulness, facts relevant to sentencing) or in which it is helpful to give background on scientific, technical, or administrative issues, you have a fair degree of freedom in sequencing the topics.

Alternatively, you can, for a subject that relates only to a single argument, place a background statement about that discrete subject immediately before the argument to which it relates. For example, in an appellate brief challenging as one of several errors the trial court's exclusion of testimony of a witness, you may precede the argument with a mini-procedural history describing the context in which the proffered testimony arose; the proffered testimony itself; the arguments for and against exclusion; and the basis for the trial court's ruling excluding it. Such a narrative might appear under an argument subheading A entitled '*The Trial Court's Exclusion of Witness Y's Testimony*.' Argument subheading B would then be entitled '*The Trial Court Erred in Excluding Witness Y's Testimony*,' and the argument would then unfold. For some arguments, the relevant facts may be so few and simple that the narrative may simply appear, without a separate heading, as the first or second paragraph in the argument. This paragraph should be akin to a purely instructional paragraph; it should not contain any argumentative language:

> *Appellant challenges the trial court's decision not to instruct the jury on the elements of manslaughter. The trial court declined to instruct the jury on manslaughter because it understood the holding of State v. Workman to require such an instruction only if the "defendant's actions constituted a disregard of, without extreme indifference to, a substantial risk that a homicide may occur." According to the trial court, no rational jury that concluded that Appellant had caused the victim's death could also conclude that Appellant's actions met that standard. The standard of review for the trial court's decision is abuse of discretion.*

In this four-sentence paragraph, the two interior sentences are, in essence, a little background statement that sets forth procedural facts relevant only to the argument that follows.

This modular approach to background statements relevant to only one argument of several is easy on the judge's short-term memory. He gets the facts when he needs them and not a moment sooner. And their placement in a standalone subsection within a discrete argument gives him the comfort of knowing that once he has finished reading that argument and resolved it, he may put the facts from that subsection out of his mind. That stands in contrast with the facts in the background statements preceding the argument section. For those, the judge will naturally read them on the working assumption that he will need to keep all those facts in his mind as he works his way through the various arguments in the brief. For this reason, you should be open to making liberal use of modular statements. Although they do not necessarily yield shorter briefs, they do allow you to get to your argument sooner. This will fight against the judge's perception, unfair as it often is, that you are burdening him with "unnecessary" facts and "taking too long" to get to your point.

When to Outline and Draft a Background Statement: Because background statements appear before arguments, most lawyers draft them before they draft their arguments. That, however, is not an inevitable choice. You might first consider how confidently and fully you know the facts the statement concerns.

If you think you have a strong command of the facts—as at, for example, the summary judgment or trial phase, after discovery has concluded—consider drafting the background statement only after you have written or at least fully outlined the argument. That will identify for you those facts that are necessary to your argument and those that are extraneous.

By contrast, at the outset of a case or, worse, if you just joined a case long after it began, consider drafting the background statement first. Drafting the statement first is the surest, most efficient way to learn the case. And if possible, run it by a supportive co-counsel with a deeper knowledge of the case before you turn to the argument, to see if you have made mistakes or left out anything important. This will make it easier for you to draft the argument. And if, after you draft the argument, you find that you included extraneous facts in your draft of the background statement, you can edit them out then.

No matter when you draft a background statement, the advice to prepare an outline first applies as strongly as it would to drafting an argument; but with an important modification. The traditional, multi-level structure of an outline is rarely a good fit for narration. For that, a simple chronology, with indented subordinate bullet points identifying the details to bring out for each event or item on the timeline, is likely to be more helpful.

* * *

Background statements cast lawyers in a teaching role throughout whose performance they must remain in character. An unrelentingly neutral, non-argumentative tone, coupled with logical organization, will, even more perhaps than good word choice and style, favorably predispose the judge to your ensuing arguments. More important, it will invest you with the reserves of credibility upon which you will later draw as you advance those arguments with zeal. Appearing early in a brief, background statements give you an irreplaceable opportunity to make a good early impression on the judge. Seize it.

AFTERWORD

How to Get Better

Legal writing is one of the many skills that resist complete instruction. At some point, improvement comes solely from within. This afterword identifies three things that will help you get better on your own. Each focuses on an attitude you should bring to your professional writing. Your attitudes reflect your motivations, and when you are trying to get better at something, your motivations sometimes influence the outcome as much as talent and hard work. Attitude adjustment will also be a focus here because legal writing is, except in rare cases, collaborative. Whether you work in a law firm or a government office, or even if you become an appellate judge, writing collaboratively is a professional imperative.

1. Accept Criticism Graciously and Gratefully . . . : "'People ask . . . for criticism, but they only want praise.'" *Campbell v. Acuff-Rose Music, Inc.*, 510 U.S. 569, 592 (1994), quoting W. Somerset Maugham, *Of Human Bondage* (1915). But whether or not you want criticism, you are going to get it. If you are an associate at a law firm, you will get it from partners; if you are a partner, you will get it from other partners and co-counsel (and sometimes, most valuably, from associates with commendable bravery). Worst of all, criticism will come from clients who, rightly or wrongly, think that your written product is not up to snuff. When this criticism comes, as it will, repress the urge to push back and challenge it. There is a time and a way to stand your ground and defend your draft, but only after you have dispassionately considered the critic's comments. Comments that at first seem misguided may harbor important insights that your closeness to the draft hid from you. Either way, find a way to express gratitude to your reviewers sincerely and without unctuousness. Your professional reputation or even survival may depend on it.

2. . . . But Don't Just Assume It's Right: But do not assume the criticism is well founded. No matter where you work, poor advice on legal writing abounds, and if you slavishly follow it, your writing will suffer. You have to somehow develop the ability to distinguish good suggestions from bad; and then, depending on your assessment of the politics of your workplace, either disregard the bad or hold your nose and take them. A young lawyer might reasonably ask, *How can I tell a good suggestion from a bad?* That can indeed be hard. Hopefully, if you have read this far, you have learned not only advice to follow but also advice to shun. *E.g.*, *Always keep your sentences short*; *Never use the passive voice*; *Get rid of all adverbs*; *Make the statement of facts an integral part of your argument*; *Try to grab the judge in the very first sentence*; *Make the first paragraph of your argument a summary of the argument to come*; *Use all caps for high-level argument headings*. Beyond that, you just have to rely on your own judgment and, to a lesser extent, the esteem in which the adviser's own writing is held by colleagues you respect.

Yet by far, the most important advice for getting better is: *Give a damn*.

3. Give a Damn: If you want to get better at writing, you have to want to get better. When your desire to improve is strong and sincere, it expresses itself in two ways.

The first way in which your desire to improve expresses itself is by cringing at the prospect of giving anyone a rough draft of anything. Whenever you share a draft with a colleague, a supervisor, or, above all, a client, that typo-free draft should be the best you know how to produce. For when you go to a reader with the windup *This is just a first/rough draft . . .* , you implicitly send the message that you are not a full professional. And no reader, even the kindest, can help but ask herself, when presented with such a draft, *Why then should I read this draft now?* Maybe there is a good answer. Maybe the reader asked for the draft in its current state because she would not have time to review it later; maybe the drafter is stuck on a question only the reader can answer after reading the draft in full; maybe the drafter suffered a power outage and the battery on his laptop is running low. But otherwise, the only reasons that suggest themselves are that the drafter started drafting too late to complete a polished first draft or that he did not care enough to polish it. (Or, perhaps, like the law office scrivener, Bartleby, whom Melville memorably portrayed, he just "would prefer not to.") The need to make the first draft you circulate as good as it can be becomes all the more compelling when you come to realize, as you will, that the first circulated draft, not later, typically draws the most careful review from clients and co-counsel. Failing to provide them with polished first drafts can cause them to lose confidence in you prematurely.

The second, related way in which your desire to improve expresses itself is by caring as much about how something is said as about whether it is true or just. That might strike you as odd in the context of legal writing. If it does, that is good. For if the rule of law means anything, it means that cases should be decided on their merits; not because one side's lawyer knows how to use the passive voice effectively or how to vary sentence length nearly as well as Oliver Wendell Holmes. But to say that truth and justice matter more than style—they do, by far—is not to say that lawyers who care far more about the content of their writing than about its style can become very good legal writers. They probably cannot because they will just not have the patience to engage in the ruthless self-criticism and self-editing that good writing requires. Passable writers are probably the most such lawyers can aspire to become.

Their apathy does not make them bad litigators or doom them to failure in the profession. Many great trial lawyers are not good writers, perhaps because they have suppressed the urge to successively self-edit. In court, that would make them stutter. There may also be a tension between the self-confidence that helps so many lawyers succeed and the self-doubt that fuels the urge to self-edit. But if you do have these urges to improve and refine, all sourced from an aesthetic drive to make every sentence better, then you have, with help from this book, a clear path to successful legal writing and to places within the profession that reward that skill.

ADDITIONAL MATERIALS

General References on Writing

The following general references on writing are useful:

For basic grammatical concepts and rules: *Rules of English: Understanding Grammar, in* NEW OXFORD AMERICAN DICTIONARY 1962–85 (Oxford Univ. Press 2d ed. 2005).

For punctuation, capitalization, and other typographical matters: THE CHICAGO MANUAL OF STYLE (Univ. of Chicago Press) (any recent edition).

For advanced grammar and usage: BRYAN A. GARNER, GARNER'S MODERN AMERICAN USAGE (Oxford Univ. Press 2003).

For sentence and paragraph construction: JOSEPH M. WILLIAMS, STYLE: TEN LESSONS IN CLARITY AND GRACE (Scott, Foresman 3d ed. 1989).

For fun: H.W. FOWLER, A DICTIONARY OF MODERN ENGLISH USAGE (Oxford Univ. Press 1944).

A Classification System for Contentions

Here is a classification system for legal and factual contentions more detailed than the system offered in Chapter 6 (The Order of Paragraphs). The system identifies the types of legal and factual contentions that appear in U.S. legal analysis and groups them according to the degree to which they relate to one another.

1. Legal
   - 1.1 Interpretive
     - 1.1.1 Definitional Meaning
       - 1.1.1.1 Dictionary (current [*i.e.*, "plain meaning"] or historical)
       - 1.1.1.2 Statutory, Regulatory, or Contractual Definition
     - 1.1.2 Logical Meaning (*e.g.*, contrary interpretation "proves too much")
     - 1.1.3 Intended Meaning
       - 1.1.3.1 Purpose of legal source
       - 1.1.3.2 Legislative history (constitution, statute, rule, regulation)
       - 1.1.3.3 Drafting history (contract, will, trust)
       - 1.1.3.4 Adversarial admission (*e.g.*, after contract execution; in litigation)
     - 1.1.4 Contextual Meaning
       - 1.1.4.1 Within sentence
       - 1.1.4.2 Within paragraph/section
       - 1.1.4.3 Within statute/set of regulations
       - 1.1.4.4 Within body of law as a whole (*e.g.*, related statutes, regulations, field of law)
     - 1.1.5 Interpreted Meaning
       - 1.1.5.1 Judicial (in instant case; if in different, *see* 1.2)
       - 1.1.5.2 Expert

1.2 Precedential

1.2.1 Result Supported/Not Supported by Controlling or Persuasive Case Law

1.2.2 Result Supported/Not Supported by Similarity of Instant Case's Facts to Facts of Controlling or Persuasive Case Law

1.3 Prudential/Policy/Pragmatic

1.3.1 More Efficient: creates better incentives for behavior

1.3.1.1 In court (*i.e.*, procedural arguments)

1.3.1.2 In human society

1.3.2 More Just

1.3.2.1 Avoids result in instant case that would offend sense of fairness or that would be absurd

1.3.2.2 Avoids result in future cases that would offend sense of fairness or that would be absurd (*e.g.*, slippery slope arguments)

2. Factual

2.1 Indisputable

2.1.1 Facts Assumed for Purposes of Decision Because of Standard of Decision (*e.g.*, on motion to dismiss)

2.1.2 Prior Ruling Establishes Fact

2.1.2.1 Prior ruling in same case (*e.g.*, on remand)

2.1.2.2 Prior ruling in different case involving the same parties (*i.e.*, issue preclusion)

2.1.3 Unrebuttable Presumption Establishes Fact

2.2 Uncontradicted

2.2.1 Evidence in Record Demonstrates Fact and No Evidence Contradicts It

2.2.2 Fact Admitted by Adversary

2.3 Contradicted/Ambiguous

2.3.1 Weight: conflict in evidence should be resolved in favor of more plausible finding

2.3.2 Credibility: conflict in evidence should be resolved by rejecting evidence that is not credible

2.3.3 Reliability: conflict in evidence should be resolved by rejecting evidence that is not reliable

2.3.4 Rebuttable Presumption: conflict in evidence should be resolved in accord with presumption not rebutted by other considerations (weight, credibility, reliability)

In the style of the Linnaean taxonomical system, each type of contention will be referred to as a class (Level 1), a genus (Level 2), a species (Level 3), or a subspecies (Level 4), depending on the level it occupies.

1. Legal Contentions: Within the class of legal contentions, the system recognizes three genera: **interpretive**, **precedential**, and **prudential**.

Interpretive: An interpretive contention is any reason why a legal source should carry a certain meaning. "Legal source" means the public (*e.g.*, constitution, statute, rule, regulation, order, patent claim) or private (*e.g.*, contract, will, trust) text that states the legal rule whose application or non-application the argument seeks.

The simplest case is one in which the parties do not dispute the meaning of the legal source. In, say, a case in which the question is whether a person drove through a red light, the meaning of a "red light" under the governing law is highly unlikely to be disputed. In such an extreme case, one of the legal contentions on which the argument is based is so fundamental and obvious (*viz.*, '*A red light means a traffic light emitting light with a wavelength between approximately 620 nm and 740 nm.*') that it will not even be stated. But strictly speaking, such an implicit contention is interpretive. More specifically, this implicit contention falls within the species of interpretive contentions classified as "definitional meaning." (1.1.1) Contentions based on definitional meaning—sometimes referred to as "plain meaning" or "dictionary meaning"—are ubiquitous.

More complex, interesting species of interpretive contentions are those classified as "logical," "intended," and "contextual." Extended discussion of these types of contentions falls outside the scope of this book, whose focus is practice, not jurisprudence. Hopefully, the terms used to denote these species and their subspecies are sufficiently familiar to enable the law student or lawyer to classify contentions according to them without difficulty. If not, review of books on jurisprudence or interpretation may be helpful.[1]

The fifth species of interpretive contentions, "interpreted meaning," is also familiar, but some discussion focused on its two subspecies is appropriate.

a. An interpreted meaning contention that is "judicial" means a legal contention based on a ruling by the court in the instant case. A common example is a ruling based on a partial summary judgment or, in patent cases, a ruling construing the meaning of terms in patent claims.

b. An interpreted meaning contention that is "expert" means an opinion of an expert about the meaning of a legal source. Most commonly these come from secondary sources, such as treatises or law review articles. Occasionally retained experts offer opinions on the meaning of legal sources, most commonly patent claims or foreign laws.[2] Far more commonly, however, retained experts submit opinions on disputed facts. As such, their opinions should be classified as factual, not legal, contentions.

Precedential: In the more common situation in which you are relying on the holdings of different, prior cases to contend that a legal source, public or private, has a certain meaning, then the contention falls within the second genus of legal contentions: precedential. These types of contentions, for which Anglo-American jurisprudence is famous, have two species: those that draw upon the closeness of the principle they state or the interpretation they advance to the principle or interpretation you advance; and those that draw upon a similarity of facts in the instant and precedential cases. The two species are not truly exclusive. A particularly strong case may be both. That is not a flaw in the classification system, nor does this duality complicate outlining. If you have such a doubly powerful case on your

---

1. *E.g.*, Edward H. Levi, An Introduction to Legal Reasoning (Univ. of Chicago Press 1949); Ward Farnsworth, The Legal Analyst (Univ. of Chicago Press 2007); Antonin Scalia & Bryan A. Garner, Reading Law (West 2011). The discussion in the latter of the many "syntactic," "contextual," and "semantic" canons may be especially helpful for developing and classifying interpretive contentions.

2. Expert opinions on foreign law present a special classification issue. A purist might classify them as factual contentions, but there are settings in which you may wish to present them in the context of your interpretive, legal contentions.

side, you will want to feature it early in the part of your argument dedicated to precedential contentions, possibly even before you lay out your interpretive contentions.

The system does not distinguish precedential contentions based on controlling authority from those based on authority that is merely persuasive. Although such contentions have different force, they are analytically identical.

Prudential: The third, final genus of legal contentions is prudential contentions, also referred to as policy or pragmatic contentions. These are contentions that derive their force from the notion that, all other things being equal, the interpretation of legal sources should further human welfare. Or at least it should not lead to inefficient, unfair, or absurd results. Prudential contentions often resemble the first subspecies of intended meaning contentions: those based on the purpose of the legal source being interpreted. (1.1.3.1) But they differ from purposive contentions because the purpose of an enactment or provision is generally self-evident, whereas prudential contentions generally call for more extended explanation. For example, the clear purpose of the First Amendment's provision that "Congress shall make no law . . . abridging the freedom of speech" is to ensure that federal statutes do not censor forms of expression classified as speech. That is an interpretive contention. (1.1.3.1) By contrast, the contention that the Free Speech Clause should not be interpreted to cover flag-burning because burning flags creates risks of arson and other physical dangers not presented by other forms of expressive conduct is prudential. (1.3.1.2)

2. Factual: The classification system recognizes three genera of factual contentions.

Indisputable: The first genus comprises factual contentions advanced in contexts in which the facts to be applied are indisputable. A fact is indisputable when it has already been the subject of findings or when an unrebuttable legal presumption or standard of decision requires your adversary to accept the fact as true. For example, on a motion to dismiss, the movant must accept the facts pleaded in the complaint. In such a setting, the non-movant's factual contentions will generally be in the perfunctory form, e.g., '*Because the complaint alleges X, the Court must, in evaluating this motion, take X as true.*' Factual contentions concerning indisputable facts will rarely be more elaborate unless the governing legal standard or presumption is contested. If so, the contention setting forth why the standard or presumption does not apply is legal, not factual.

Uncontradicted: The second genus comprises factual contentions advanced in contexts in which the contended facts are uncontradicted. A fact is uncontradicted either when it has been admitted or when you are confident your adversary will not contest it because no evidence in the record contradicts it.

Contradicted/Ambiguous: The most common and by far most interesting genus of factual contentions is the third: contradicted/ambiguous. These are the contentions that dominate closing arguments at trials and that rarely show up in appellate arguments. In practice, the difference between contradictory evidence and ambiguous evidence is often muddy. Fortunately, the distinction is not important in outlining the factual contentions you will make to advance your client's position on the contested fact. The four species falling within this genus are familiar and do not require explanation.

Index

adjectives, 48–49
adverbs, 12–13, 28, 49–50
allusions, to facts, 149–151
argument(s)
 breadth of, 2, 131, 133
 contentions in, 101
 defined, 101–103
 impact of, 2, 131
 order of, 2, 129–136
 order of paragraphs in, 2
 parallel, in table of contents, 144–145
 in teach first-argue later, 103–127
 viability of, 2, 131–132
argument headers, 90–91

background statements
 argumentativeness in, 154–155
 likability and, 153–154
 order of, 169–172
 order of paragraphs in, 160–169
 order of sentences in paragraphs of, 157–160
 pedagogy in, 155–156
 teaching in, 155–156
 word order in sentences of, 156–157
breadth, of arguments, 2, 131, 133
breaks, paragraph, 91
brief, order of arguments in, 2

cases, placement of factually similar, 122–124
clichéd metaphors, 70
compound entries, in table of contents, 147–149
Conclusion–Rule–Proof-of-Rule–Application–Conclusion (CRuPAC), 126
contention(s)
 ambiguous factual, 120–121, 184
 in arguments, 101–102, 110–111
 classification of, 179–184
 contradicted factual, 120–121, 180–181, 184
 factual, 100, 110–111, 119–122, 180–181, 183–184
 grouping of related, 113
 indisputable factual, 120, 180, 183–184
 interpretive, 115–117, 179, 181–182
 legal, 100, 110–111, 179–183
 precedential, 117, 180, 182–183
 prudential, 116–118, 180, 183
 related, 119–122
 uncontradicted factual, 120, 180, 184
 undisputed interpretive, 114–115
context, factual, in table of contents, 149–152
credibility, 61
criticism, taking, 173–174
CRuPAC. *See* Conclusion–Rule–Proof-of-Rule–Application–Conclusion (CRuPAC)

decision tree, in table of contents, 137–143
diction, 62–63
double subject-blockers, 13–16

efficiency, of sentences, 5–35

facts, allusions to, 149–151
factual context, in table of contents, 149–152
false paragraph breaks, 91

idea, most important, for persuasion, 39–44
impact, of arguments, 2, 131
IRAC. *See* Issue–Rule–Application–Conclusion (IRAC)
Issue–Rule–Application–Conclusion (IRAC), 126

length, sentence, 93–94
likability, 153–154
Litigation English, 63–64
lookback, 51–52

metaphors, clichéd, 70
multiple-negative constructions, 28–29
must, should *vs.*, 147

negatives, multiple, 28–29
nominalization-preposition mismatch, 69–70
nominalizations, 25–28
nouns, descriptive proper, in table of contents, 151–152

objects, 45
ordinals, 56–58

paragraph(s)
  affirmative, 2, 72–75, 79–80
  arguing, 105–106
  argument in, 101–103
  classification of, according to purpose, 72–77
  coherence of, 92
  defined, 71
  factually similar cases in, 122–124
  false breaks, 91
  history of, 71
  instructional, 2, 72–73, 78–79
  order of, 2, 99–127, 160–169
  order of sentences in, 2, 71–97, 157–160
  rebuttal placement in, 124–126
  responsive, 2, 72, 75–77, 81–85
  roadmap, 107–109
  starting, 78–91
  teach first-argue later in, 103–127
  teaching, 105–106
parallel arguments, 144–145
parallel construction, 6, 32–35
participial phrases, 8–9
passive voice, 145–146
persuasiveness
  adjectives in, 48–49
  adverbs in, 49–50
  beginning of sentence in, 50–58
  credibility and, 61
  end of sentence in, 38–50
  identification of most important idea for, 39–44
  lookback in, 51–52
  middle of sentence in, 58–59
  objects in, 45
  ordinals in, 56–58
  sentence connection in, 51–56
  with sentences, 37–70
  subjects in, 46–47
  subordinate clauses in, 52–53
  topic identification in, 50–51
  verbs in, 47–48
prepositional phrases, 10–11
professionalism
  diction in, 62–63
  sentences for, 61–70

pronouns
- demonstrative, 19–20
- personal, 17–18
- possessive, 19
- relative, 20–22
- unambiguous use of, 6, 17–22

rebuttal placement, 124–126

sentence(s)
- beginning of, 50–58
- connection, 51–56
- denial, 82–85
- double subject-blockers in, 13–16
- efficient, 5–35
- end of, 38–50
- length, 93–94
- middle of, 58–59
- order of, in paragraph, 2, 71–97, 157–160
- persuasive, 37–70
- professional, 61–70
- sprawl in, 94–97
- starter, 2, 78–81, 86–90
- target, 81–82
- topic identification in, 50–51
- word order in, 1–2, 156–157

should, must *vs.*, 147
sprawl, in sentences, 94–97
subjects, 46–47
subject-verb mismatch, 64, 66–67
subordinate clauses, 52–53

table of contents
- allusions to facts in, 149–151
- compound entries in, 147–149
- decision tree in, 137–143
- descriptive proper nouns in, 151–152
- factual context in, 149–152
- parallel arguments in, 144–145
- passive voice in, 145–146
- purpose of, 137
- statement of reasons in, 143–144

teach first-argue later (TFAL), 103–127
TFAL. *See* teach first-argue later (TFAL)
topic identification, 50–51

verb-object mismatch, 65, 67–69
verb-preposition mismatch, 65, 69–70
verbs, 47–48
viability, of arguments, 2, 131–132
voice, passive, 145–146

word order, in sentences, 1–2, 156–157
words
- adverbs, 12–13
- in excess verbiage, 22–25
- moving, to end of sentence, 44–50
- necessary, 6, 30–32
- as nominalizations, 25–28
- in participial phrases, 8–9
- in prepositional phrases, 10–11
- related, 6–16
- as traffic signals, 53–56
- unnecessary, 6, 22–29